## Presented to:

Matthew Lee

## By:

Faith Church

## Occasion:

Pre-K Graduation

## Date:

June 7, 2024

*May the stories in this Bible help to remind you of how much God loves you.*

# The Spark Story Bible

Presented to

_____

By

_____

Date

_____

# THE SPARK STORY BIBLE

## Spark a Journey through God's Word

Edited by Debra Thorpe Hetherington

Illustrated by Peter Grosshauser
and Ed Temple

SPARK
HOUSE
FAMILY

MINNEAPOLIS

First edition published 2015
Printed in China

24 23    7 8 9

ISBN:   978-1-4514-9978-0    Hard cover

ISBN: 978-1-4514-9979-7    E-book

Illustrations: Peter Grosshauser and Ed Temple
Book design: Eileen Z. Engebretson
Contributors: Patti Thisted Arthur, Kari Bahe, Carolyn Banks, Becky Weaver Carlson, Erin Gibbons, Barbara DeGrote, Debra Thorpe Hetherington, Melanie Heuiser Hill, Diane Jacobson, Kimberly Leetch, Mary C. Lindberg, Tera Michelson, Debbie Trafton O'Neal, Cynthia Fairman Paulson, Diana Running, Cheryl Mulberry, Sue Tornai, Kathy Donlan Tunseth, Joe Vaughan, Mary Ingram Zentner
Cover design: Alisha Lofgren

Library of Congress Cataloging-in-Publication Data

The spark story Bible : spark a journey through God's word / [editor], Debra Thorpe Hetherington ; illustrations, Peter Grosshauser and Ed Temple.
    pages cm
  Audience: Ages 3-7.
  Audience: K to grade 3.
  ISBN 978-1-4514-9978-0 (alk. paper)
1. Bible stories, English. I. Hetherington, Debra Thorpe, editor. II. Grosshauser, Peter, illustrator. III. Temple, Ed, illustrator.
  BS551.3.S63 2015
  220.95'05--dc23
                            2015010809

Printed on acid-free paper.

VN0006065; 9781451499780; MAY2023

Sparkhouse Family
PO Box 1209
Minneapolis, MN 55440-1209
sparkhouse.org

# Welcome to The Spark Story Bible!

Imagine what it was like when the world was being created. Count the stars in the sky with Abram and Sarai as they learn about God's astonishing promise. Be amazed with the shepherds and angels when Jesus is born. Wonder about what it was like to look into the empty tomb with the women on Easter morning.

Exploring *The Spark Story Bible* is the perfect way for children and adults to get to know the Bible together from beginning to end. Experience something new each time you read a story, either through the words of the story, the creative art, or the suggested activities and discussion questions.

Be sure to watch for Squiggles, the expressive caterpillar whose response to each story will help spark children's engagement with the story.

Grow in faith together as you explore and talk about God's Word.

# Stories from the Old Testament

# Stories from the New Testament

# Creation

Before God created the world, there was nothing at all—except God.

On the first day
of creation, the wind
of God blew. WHISH!
WOOSH! SWOOSH! God said,
"Let there be light!" CRACKLE! BOOM! BANG!
There was light. God saw that the light was
good. Then, SPLLLLLITTT! God divided the
light and the darkness into day and night.
On the second day, God said, "Let there be a
sky!" PILLOW! BILLOW! PUFF! There was a sky.
God saw that the sky was good.

On the third day,

God said, "Let there

be water and dry land!"

DRIP! DROP! KERPLUNK!

There was water.

CRACKLE! CRUNCH! SNAP!

There was dry land. God saw that

the water and land were good.

Then God said, "Let there be

plants and trees!" RUMBLE!

RUSTLE! POP!

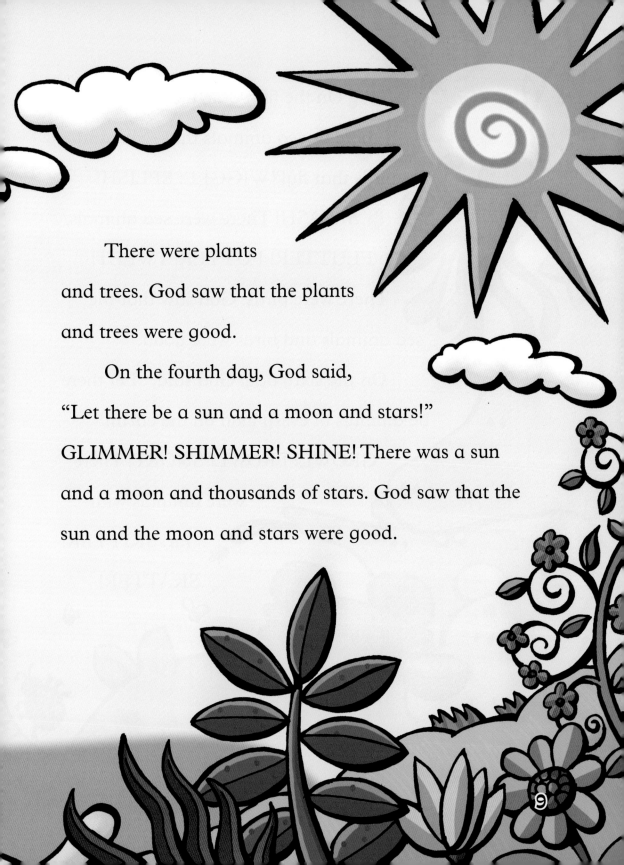

There were plants
and trees. God saw that the plants
and trees were good.

On the fourth day, God said,
"Let there be a sun and a moon and stars!"
GLIMMER! SHIMMER! SHINE! There was a sun
and a moon and thousands of stars. God saw that the
sun and the moon and stars were good.

On the fifth day, God said, "Let there be sea animals that swim and birds that fly!" WIGGLE! SPLISH! SPLASH! There were sea animals. FLUTTER! PUTTER! TWEET! There were birds. God saw that the sea animals and birds were good.

On the sixth day, God said, "Let there be animals of every kind on the earth!" GROWL! PROWL! SNORT! There were animals with fur. SKITTER! SKATTER!

CREEP! There were bugs. SLITHER, SLINK, HOP! There were reptiles.

God saw that the animals and bugs and reptiles were good. Then God said, "Let there be people on the earth!" BLINK! WINK! HICCUP! There were people on the earth. God saw that the people were very good.

On the seventh day, God said, "It is time to rest!" WHEW! PSHEW! AHHH! God and all of creation rested.

Go outside into God's creation. Look around—God made it all! Say a prayer, thanking God for all of creation.

11

# Adam and Eve

After creating the whole world, God looked around and was very happy. It was an incredible world filled with wonderful animals, plants, and included two very special people—a man and a woman.

God made a beautiful place for the man and woman to live, an amazing garden. God named the man Adam and the woman Eve.

God said to Adam and Eve, "I need someone to help me take care of this amazing world! Will you help me?"

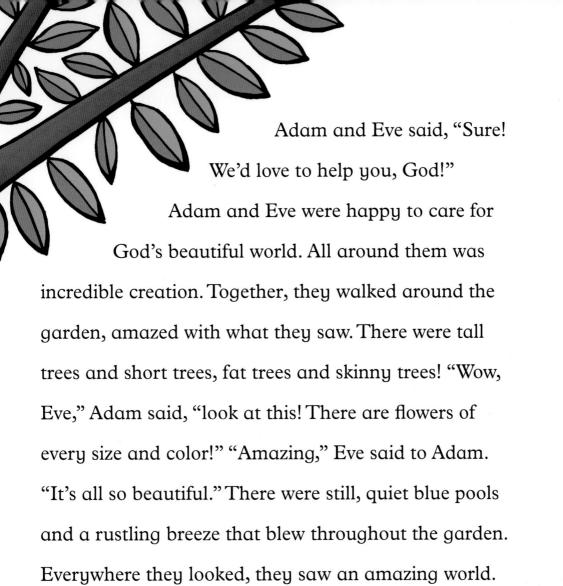

Adam and Eve said, "Sure!
We'd love to help you, God!"
Adam and Eve were happy to care for
God's beautiful world. All around them was
incredible creation. Together, they walked around the
garden, amazed with what they saw. There were tall
trees and short trees, fat trees and skinny trees! "Wow,
Eve," Adam said, "look at this! There are flowers of
every size and color!" "Amazing," Eve said to Adam.
"It's all so beautiful." There were still, quiet blue pools
and a rustling breeze that blew throughout the garden.
Everywhere they looked, they saw an amazing world.

When she looked at all of the animals God placed in the garden—the ones that fluttered through the sky, the ones that wiggled and squirmed across the ground, and the ones that frolicked and played across the land—Eve said, "It's going to be hard to keep track of them all!"

"Don't worry, Eve," Adam said, "God asked me to give all the animals names to help us keep track and take care of them all—this is toucan and chickadee and monkey and squirrel."

"This tall, tall creature is called giraffe! The silly one with a long nose—she will be an elephant! And this one who wags his tail will be dog," Adam said. "Look how he follows me wherever I go!"

16

God watched over Adam and Eve as Adam shared all the names of the animals while they played with them in the garden. God was happy to see that Adam and Eve were taking such good care of everything in creation.

What are some of **YOUR** favorite things that God created? Ask your family members what their favorite things are. How many are the same as yours?

17

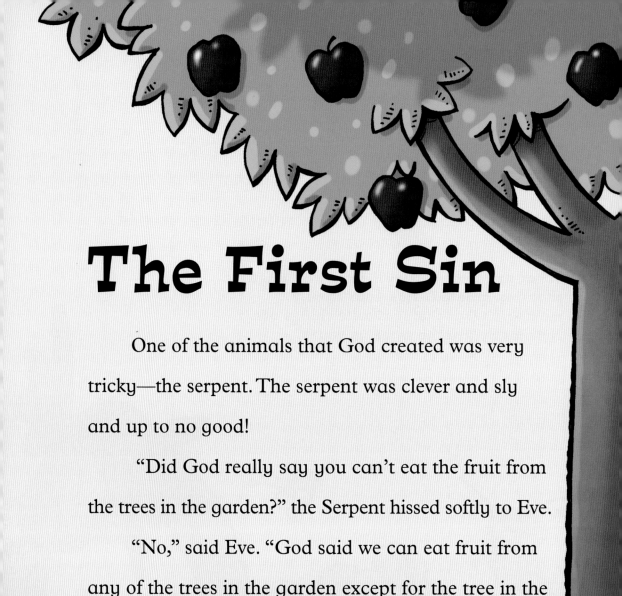

# The First Sin

One of the animals that God created was very tricky—the serpent. The serpent was clever and sly and up to no good!

"Did God really say you can't eat the fruit from the trees in the garden?" the Serpent hissed softly to Eve.

"No," said Eve. "God said we can eat fruit from any of the trees in the garden except for the tree in the middle of the garden. God said not to eat from that one—not to even touch it."

The serpent smiled
a sneaky little smile.
"Ha! God doesn't want
you to eat fruit from that tree because if you do,
you'll know everything—you'll be just like God!" the
serpent hissed in his sly way.

Eve looked at the
tree in the middle.
Hmmm . . . the fruit
sure looked good!

So she ate some. And she
gave some to Adam, too.

As soon as they ate

the fruit, EVERYTHING

CHANGED. Adam and Eve became very embarrassed
and shy. They sewed some leaves together, making
some pretend clothes to try to cover up their bodies.
They stood nervously behind some bushes.

Then, they heard God walking
around in the garden. God called
out to them, "Yoo-hoo! Where
are you?"

Adam and Eve hid.

"Hey! Where did you go?" called God.

Adam peeked out from behind some vines. He said, "I heard you . . . and I was afraid."

"Why were you afraid?" asked God.

"Well, I'm naked, for one thing," said Adam, who was quite embarrassed. "So I hid."

"I see," God replied. "Who told you that you were naked?" Adam said nothing.

"Did you eat fruit from the tree I told you not to eat from?" asked God.

"Eve gave it to me!" Adam blurted out.

"The serpent made me!" exclaimed Eve. "He *tricked* me!"

God sighed. "I told you not to eat from that tree. Because you have done what I told you not to do, life will be difficult for you now. You will have to leave this beautiful garden and work very hard to get the things you need.

Now you will know what it is to be unhappy. And someday, you will die. I made you from dust. When you die you will become dust again."

God made some real clothes for Adam and Eve and sent them out into the big world. And God was with them everywhere they went.

What kinds of hard work do you think Adam and Eve will have to do out in the world?

# Noah's Ark

A long time passed since God created the world. People forgot about God except for one man. His name was Noah. He loved and obeyed God.

"I am very sad that people have forgotten about me," God said to Noah.

"I am going to bring rain to flood the earth—lots and lots of rain. Build yourself a huge boat of cypress wood." Noah did just what God said and made a big, big boat with lots of rooms.

Noah was 600 years old when he entered the boat with his wife, their sons, and their sons' wives. God brought two of every kind of animal to the boat.

Elephants and zebras, lions and tigers, pigs
and giraffes, dogs and cats, deer and rhinos,
bears and cows, horses and goats, lambs and
monkeys all came two by two. All different
kinds of animals, birds, and creepy, crawly things came
to the boat. Noah took all of them into the boat.
Then the door shut behind them.

Inside the big boat the lions roared,
the dogs barked, and the birds chirped.

It was stuffy and stinky! It was muggy and hot!
On the outside it rained and rained.

It rained big, giant drops and little, baby drops for
40 days and 40 nights. The rains came down and the
flood waters came up. The water splashed on the sides
of the big boat and pushed it up and down for 150 days.
Finally it rested on the top of a tall mountain.

Noah waited and waited until God said to him, "Come out of the boat, you and your wife and your sons and their wives." Noah's family and all the animals came off the boat.

They put their feet on dry land. They ran, and skipped, and jumped. They twirled and danced in the sunlight. They thanked God for the land and God blessed them. Noah's family grew and grew. The animals and the birds and the creepy crawly things filled the earth again.

God painted a rainbow of brilliant red, orange, yellow, green, blue, and violet across the sky and promised, "Never again will water flood the earth. Whenever you see the rainbow in the clouds, I will see it too, and I will remember."

What would you have thought if God asked you to build a boat? What would you have said to God?

29

# Abram's Call

One day God said to a man named Abram, "It's time for you to leave your home and family and go to a new land! In this new land I will give you many things and make sure people know about you. I will be kind to those who are kind to you. To the ones who are unkind, I will be unkind. Because of you, all the families on earth will be blessed."

Abram was 75 years old and had a long white beard. But he didn't let his age stop him! On his trip Abram took his wife, Sarai, and his nephew Lot. They walked the many miles leading to the new land. It was a hot and dusty trip, but Abram knew that where God was leading them would be a beautiful place. The trip was long and hard because they carried all their pots and pans, dishes and clothes with them.

"Whew! I'm hot," said Sarai as her face grew red.

"I'm getting kind of tired," sighed Abram.

"My feet hurt!" groaned Lot.

When they finally got to the land of
Canaan, Abram stopped by a tall and shady
oak tree. It felt good to get out of the blazing sun.
God came to him there in the cool shade and said,

"I have a surprise for you. I promise to give this land to your family forever!"

Abram and Sarai and Lot were so thankful to God for this wonderful gift they jumped and danced and hugged each other and shouted "Hurray!" To show God how grateful they were, Abram decided to build two altars to honor God. He would build one altar out of large, smooth stones by the tree and the other altar out of pieces of wood by his tent in the hills.

Pretend that you are going on a trip. Who will come with you? Draw a picture of something you will take with you on the trip.

# God's Promises
# to Abram

God came to Abram and made a promise, "Abram, you are very special to me. I will take care of you and give you lots of children and grandchildren and great-grandchildren!"

But Abram asked God many times. "Are you sure? I don't have any children yet."

God thought Abram needed something more to help him understand. So God took Abram outside and showed him the night sky. "Your family will include as many people as there are stars in the sky," God told Abram.

Abram stared up at all those stars. He couldn't begin to count all those twinkling lights. Stars and stars and stars—all around him. Abram looked up at the stars and saw God at work. Abram believed God.

35

"Now for another promise," said God to Abram.
"You will need a place for your huge family to live. I
will give you this land as I promised."

"Are you sure God?" Abram asked again.

God made a covenant with Abram, a promise that Abram would become a father and a grandfather and a great-grandfather and a great-great-grandfather and a great-great-great grandfather and on and on. And all Abram's many, many sons, daughters, grandsons, and granddaughters would live with God in the land on which Abram stood.

 Go outside at night with a friend or family member. See how many stars you can count. Remember God's promise.

# Abraham and Sarah's Visitors

When Abram was 99 years old, he and his wife, Sarai, were still waiting for God's promise of a huge family to come true. Abram was getting frustrated. He asked God, "What are you waiting for?"

God spoke to Abram, "I will keep my promise, and I will change your names. Instead of Abram, your name will be Abraham. Instead of Sarai, your wife will be Sarah."

Abraham was afraid of what God said. He thought he was too old to become the father of so many people and his wife was too old to have children. He fell on his face and peeked up with one eye. "Could God really make such a thing happen?"

Later, as Abraham was sitting by the tent, he saw three strangers walking towards him. Abraham squinted into the sun and wondered who would be visiting him on such a hot day.

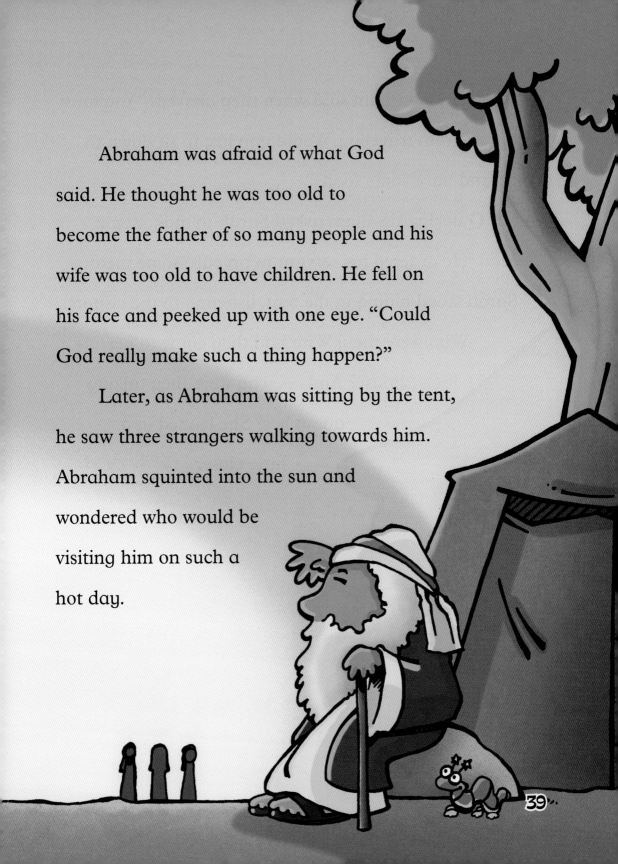

"Hi!" Abraham said when they arrived. "You must be tired from traveling. Would you like to sit down to rest and have some food?"

Quickly, Abraham asked Sarah to make some bread. He ordered his servant to prepare some meat. Sarah stood hiding in the tent, listening to the visitors. Who were they? Why had they come to her house? And . . . why were they talking about her? She leaned in a little closer . . .

"Your wife, Sarah, will have a son," the visitors said to Abraham. Sarah started to laugh. Didn't they know that she was too old to have a child? The visitors looked up. "Why is Sarah laughing?" they asked. "Doesn't she believe God's promise will happen?"

God's promise to Abraham did happen! Sarah had a baby boy and named him Isaac, which means "laughter." Abraham and Sarah's family grew and grew and grew and God blessed each generation with laughter and happiness.

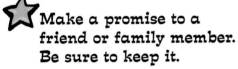

Make a promise to a
friend or family member.
Be sure to keep it.

# Rebekah and Isaac

God kept the promise to Abraham that he would have many children. God promised that Abraham's son, Isaac, would have lots of children, too. When Abraham was very old, he asked his servant to help find a wife for Isaac. The servant needed to go to a place where the people believed in God, so he went on a long, long journey to the town where Abraham grew up. When he got to the town, the servant knew that he needed to find the woman who would be Isaac's wife, but he didn't know how to find her. He prayed to God for help. He said, "God, I will go to the well in this town and ask a woman for a drink. If she gives me a drink of water and offers to get a drink for my camels, then I will know that she is the right one."

The servant waited patiently by the well. In the evening, a beautiful woman came to fill her jars with water. Her name was Rebekah. The servant asked her for a drink. Rebekah replied, "Sir, here is a drink for you. Let me get some water for your camels too."

Rebekah showed wonderful kindness. The servant believed God heard his prayer. "God sent me a very long way to find you," he told her. "God has a plan for you to marry a man named Isaac. God has promised that you and Isaac will have many children."

"I have always wanted to have a big family," Rebekah said with a smile. "I know that God keeps promises. I will marry Isaac."

After Isaac and Rebekah got married, Isaac prayed for children. Isaac and Rebekah had twin boys named Esau and Jacob. Isaac's children were Abraham's grandchildren, just like God had promised.

You are part of God's promise to Abraham too! How does that make you feel?

# Isaac's Blessing

Rebekah and Isaac asked God for a child. God gave them not one baby but two. Twins! Kick! Jab! Rebekah could feel the babies pushing and pulling on each other inside of her. "God," she prayed, "why are my babies fighting?"

"They're in a race to be born first," God answered. "Your family will be different. Your younger son will be the leader of the older one." This was a surprise to Rebekah. The oldest child was usually the leader of all of the brothers and sisters.

Wah! Esau was born first. He was hairy and red. Wah! Jacob was born next. He had smooth skin. The race was so close that Jacob was born holding onto Esau's foot.

Before long, the twins grew into men. They were very different. Esau was big and strong. Esau made Isaac very proud because he was a hunter. Jacob was smaller than Esau and very quiet. Rebekah loved that Jacob stayed around home.

When Isaac became old and blind, it was time to give his blessing to his oldest child, passing on the leadership of the family. Since Isaac couldn't see, he rubbed Esau's hairy arms to make sure he had the right son. "Esau," he said, "bring me dinner, and I will bless you." Rebekah was listening. "Jacob!" she whispered, "Hurry! Cover your arms with hairy goat skins to fool your father." Rebekah remembered that God said Jacob would make a better leader for the family than Esau. So Jacob dressed up like Esau and brought Isaac dinner. The plan worked.

Jacob tricked Isaac into making him the new leader of the family.

How would you feel if you were tricked by your brother, as Esau was?

49

# Joseph and His Brothers

Jacob lived with his family in a place called
Canaan. He had many sons! One of Jacob's younger
sons was named Joseph. Jacob spent more time with
Joseph than with his other sons. He even had a special
coat made for Joseph. It seemed to Joseph's brothers

that their father loved Joseph more than he loved them. They felt sad and angry.

One night, Joseph had a dream. The next morning he couldn't wait to tell everyone about it. "I dreamed we were all in the field tying stems of grain together. Suddenly, I couldn't believe my eyes! Your grain made a circle around mine and then bent over. You were bowing down to me! Isn't that exciting?" exclaimed Joseph.

"Our grain did what?" they laughed. "Why do you think we would bow down to you like you were some kind of king?" the brothers said angrily.

Joseph hung his head and walked away slowly and sadly.

The next night Joseph had another dream.

He excitedly told everyone about it in the morning.

"I had an even better dream last night. I looked up

into the sky and there I was! I saw the sun, the moon,

and 11 stars bow down to me. Isn't that amazing?"

he said.

This time his father was listening.

Jacob was angry with Joseph and said,

"Why do you think your mother and I would stand next

to your brothers and bow down to you as if you were

a king? I don't like the strange dreams you are having.

They will never come true!"

Now his brothers *and* his father were really mad

at him! Lucky for Joseph, Jacob decided to send his

brothers off with the sheep for a while.

Later, Jacob sent Joseph to find out how Joseph's brothers were doing with the sheep. As he was getting near them, his brothers saw him coming. "Here comes our dreaming brother. Let's get rid of him," they planned. They grabbed Joseph and threw him into a pit. Ouch! The rocks at the bottom of the pit were hard and sharp. "God, why are they doing this to me?" prayed Joseph.

A group of traders walked by on their way to Egypt. The brothers thought they'd get rid of Joseph once and for all. They sold Joseph to the traders and watched as he was taken away.

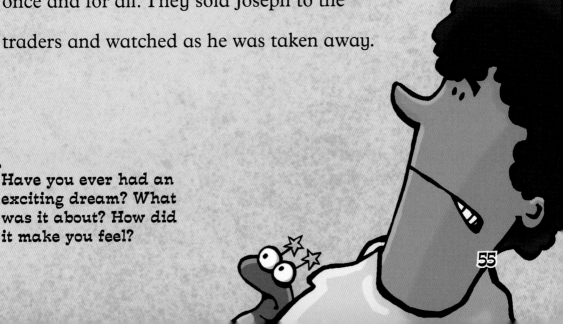

Have you ever had an exciting dream? What was it about? How did it make you feel?

55

# Pharaoh's Dreams

Joseph had many hard times. His brothers sold him to a group of traders. He was taken to Egypt, far away from his family and was put into jail—even though he hadn't done anything wrong!

Joseph thought, "How long will I be here? I didn't break any laws, but I'm in jail!" He sighed. "At least I know God will help me!"

Many months later, two men who had worked for the pharaoh were put into jail. One morning, Joseph overheard them talking. One man said, "What does it mean?" "I have no idea, but I hope I never have a dream like THAT again! It was terrible," the other man said. "Mine was, too," the first man replied.

Joseph asked, "What's wrong?" They answered, "We had weird dreams last night—we wonder what they mean!"

Joseph said, "Tell me your dreams. I can explain them!" The men described them to Joseph. God helped Joseph explain their dreams to them.

Two years later, Joseph was still in jail! One of the men Joseph had helped was with the pharaoh. Pharaoh told him, "I had a very scary dream last night! I wonder what it means!" The man remembered Joseph and told Pharaoh about Joseph's way of explaining dreams. Pharaoh asked for Joseph to be brought to him.

He told Joseph, "First I dreamed I was standing by the Nile River, and out came seven healthy, fat cows. They were eating grass, and then seven ugly, sick, skinny cows came and ate the fat cows!" The pharaoh continued, "Then, in another dream, seven plump, healthy ears of corn grew on a corn stalk. Then seven thin, rotten, unhealthy ears grew and ate the healthy ones."

God helped Joseph, and Joseph could tell the pharaoh what his dreams meant. "They mean that for seven years Egypt will have plenty of food. Then there will be seven years when there is not enough, and people will go hungry."

The pharaoh knew something had to be done! He put Joseph in charge of the whole country! Joseph saved food for seven years, getting ready for the years when there would be a shortage of food. When there

wasn't enough food in many countries, the people of Egypt had plenty! God had helped Joseph know what needed to be done. With God's help and love, Joseph did well—even through the worst of times.

How do you think Joseph knew that God loved him, even when he was in jail?

# Joseph Helps His Family

God always watched over Joseph. God spoke to Joseph in dreams, and Joseph used this knowledge to plan ahead. When the famine came, people from all over came to find food for their families because they heard that Joseph had saved up for seven years. Even Joseph's brothers traveled to Egypt to find food.

But it had been such a long time since they'd seen each other, the brothers didn't recognize Joseph!

Joseph kept the secret of who he was from his brothers for awhile. But soon he couldn't wait any longer. Joseph finally told them who he was. "I am your brother Joseph, who you sold to the Egyptian traders. Don't feel bad anymore because God sent me ahead of you so that I could save people, including you! This famine is going to last for many years, so hurry back to our father and tell him that I am safe. I want you to bring your families and your children and all of your sheep and goats to live near me!"

Once Joseph's brothers saw who he was, they all hugged each other and cried. They jumped up and down with relief and joy. Joseph and his brothers talked and talked. The brothers talked from the time the sun came up to the time the sun went down. When the pharaoh heard that Joseph's brothers had come,

he told Joseph, "Tell them to go get everyone in your family! I will give them the best land in Egypt to call their own."

Joseph gave his brothers wagons, food, and new clothes, and they went back to their father and told him the good news.

"Joseph is still alive! He is the ruler of all of Egypt!" Everyone danced when they heard the news.

"This is all I could ask for," Joseph's father said. "Now I will see my son again! Let's get moving!"

Joseph's family all moved to Egypt. But the brothers were worried, "What if Joseph is still angry with us? We were so awful to him. What can we do?"

The brothers went to Joseph and said, "Here we are—we don't deserve to be your brothers anymore, so we will be your slaves!"

But Joseph said to them, "Don't be silly! I am your brother no matter what. Even though you planned for something bad to happen to me, God turned it into something good!"

How would you have felt if you had been Joseph and were seeing your brothers after such a long time?

# Baby Moses

Pharaoh, the King of Egypt, was afraid. He was rich and powerful . . . and scared! What could he be scared of? Well, strangely enough, Pharaoh was scared of God's people, the Hebrews. He thought there were too many of them, and he was afraid that they would try to become more powerful than he was.

To make sure the Hebrews had no power, Pharaoh made them his slaves and ordered them to work very hard. Even worse, he demanded that all of the Hebrew baby boys should be drowned in the Nile River! Because of this, God's people were terribly afraid, too. Everyone in Egypt was afraid!

During this fearful time, a baby boy was born to a Hebrew mother. She loved her baby boy, and of course she wanted him to live. The baby's mother kept him safe by making a floating basket for him. She put her baby in the basket and then hid it in the water and plants at the edge of the Nile River. The baby's big sister, Miriam, hid near the shore and watched over the basket. What happened next was really amazing!

Pharaoh's daughter came down to the river to take a bath. She saw the basket among the water and plants and asked her servant to go and get it. When she opened the basket, she was surprised to see a baby boy crying.

"Hmmmm . . . This must be one of the Hebrews' children," said Pharaoh's daughter. "He's awfully cute! Wouldn't it be fun to keep him?"

"A-ha!" thought Miriam. "I can help her!" Miriam bravely stepped out of her hiding place. "I could probably find someone to help take care of the baby for you until he's a little older," she said. "That would be perfect!" said Pharaoh's daughter. Miriam was excited to tell her mother the news. The baby's mother took good care of him.

When he was old enough, he went to live with Pharaoh's daughter. Miriam and her mother prayed he would be safe with her.

"I think I will name him Moses," said Pharaoh's daughter, "because I took him out of the water."

Moses lived in Pharaoh's palace until he grew up to be a man. During that time, life became worse and worse for the Hebrews. Eventually, however, Moses helped free God's people so they could leave Egypt. Now there was something besides fear for God's people—there was HOPE!

Do an experiment: See what kinds of things float in water! What would you build a floating basket out of?

73

# The Burning Bush

Moses was watching his sheep in the hot, dry desert. Suddenly, he saw a very strange sight! Flames of fire came from a bush, but the bush did not burn up. Moses squinted his eyes. He looked around the bush one way, and he looked around the bush the other way.

"Moses! Moses!" said a loud voice. Moses was scared! "Here I am," he said.

"Take off your shoes," the voice thundered. "The place where you are standing is holy ground."

Moses kicked off his sandals, keeping his eyes on the flaming bush. "I am the God of your fathers," the voice said. Moses hid his face. He was afraid to look at God.

"I have heard my people crying in Egypt," God said. "My people are hurting and I have come to save them."

"Wow!" thought Moses. "How will God do this?"

"Go!" said God. "I am sending you to Pharaoh to ask him to let my people go."

"Me?" said Moses. "Who am I to go to Pharaoh? Who am I to lead your people?" He threw himself down onto the ground before God, but he kept one eye on the burning bush.

"I will be with you," God said.

Moses trusted God. He was willing to do everything God said. God gave Moses the words and power he needed to talk to Pharaoh and lead the people out of Egypt.

Hide behind a piece of furniture, calling, "Moses!" Have someone else play the part of Moses and then switch places.

# Free from Slavery

When Moses was alive, the Hebrew people were also called Israelites. Many Israelites were slaves in Egypt. Moses and his brother, Aaron, were their leaders and went to Pharaoh, the king of Egypt. They said, "Our God says, 'Let my people go!'"

"I don't believe in your God," shouted Pharaoh. "Now get back to work!" Hearing this, God said to Moses in a thundering voice, "Watch what I will do to Pharaoh! He will let my people go!

Tell my people, 'I will free you all and bring you back to the land I promised Abraham!'"

Because they had been slaves for so long it was hard for the people to believe Moses. So God ordered again, "Tell Pharaoh to let my people go!" Moses worried that Pharaoh might not listen to him, but Moses did what God said.

It was hard for Moses to do what God asked. What is the hardest thing you have ever had to do?

# The Plagues

God gave Moses a big job. Moses had to stand up to a very stubborn king who was making God's people work as slaves. God told Moses to go to the pharaoh and say, "Let my people go!" But Pharaoh said, "No! I will not let God's people go!" Pharaoh wanted the people to worship him, not God. So God used 10 ways, called plagues, to change Pharaoh's mind.

God turned the Nile to blood
The river began to stink
Pharaoh watched the river turn red
Knew his people could not drink
And Pharaoh still said, "No!"

God sent frogs to hop everywhere
Even into the beds
Pharaoh heard his bakers scream
When frogs jumped out of their breads
And Pharaoh still said, "No!"

God thought gnats might change Pharaoh's mind
So the people could go free
Gnats swarmed people, goats, and cows
There was no place to flee
And Pharaoh still said, "No!"

"Flies," thought God, "will do the trick"
And so God sent a zillion
Pharaoh's house filled up with flies
Outside there were a million
And Pharaoh still said, "No!"

God now struck down Pharaoh's herds
The camels all were ill
The donkeys, horses all got sick
His cows fell down, but still . . .
And Pharaoh still said, "No!"

Oozy, gooey, icky sores
On everybody's skin
God knocked and knocked on Pharaoh's heart
Pharaoh never let God in
And Pharaoh still said, "No!"

Hail pounded, thunder crashed
Pharaoh's plants laid down
Not a tree stood anywhere
All were on the ground
And Pharaoh still said, "No!"

"Let my people go," said God
Or I will send a swarm
Of locusts to devour what's left
To do your land more harm
And Pharaoh still said, "No!"

Now darkness covered Pharaoh's land
The sun did not appear
No one could move, no one could see
Still Pharaoh would not hear
And Pharaoh still said, "No!"

The last and saddest plague of all
Brought sobs throughout the lands
Parents cried as their children died
Finally, Pharaoh changed his plans
Pharaoh let God's people go.

What plague would you least like to have come to you and your family? Why?

# The Red Sea

It was a long journey leaving Egypt. The Israelites camped on the shore of the Red Sea. The people were feeling really nervous. Moses squinted into the darkening sky.

Had he heard something? Something in the distance? Moses shook his head slowly. He did not trust Pharaoh, the king of Egypt, to keep his promise.

"Do you think Pharaoh followed us?" Aaron asked. Moses stood listening. "We will see," Moses said. "We will see." Moses didn't have to wait too long.

Soon a growing cloud of dust rose up in the distance. A rumble of horse hoofs thundered toward the travelers. They could see them clearly now. Hundreds of Pharaoh's chariots charged towards them. Hundreds of soldiers followed with orders to bring the people back.

"We're trapped!" someone yelled. A strong wind began to blow. Cries went up from the people. "Moses," they shouted, "have you brought us here to die?!"

"Don't be afraid," Moses told his people. "Stand firm. God is with us."

Moses gripped the staff in his hand. "Prepare to move out!" he shouted into the wind.

"Where, Moses?" Aaron said. "There is no place to go!"

"Through the Red Sea," Moses said. "God will make a way."

Moses stood on the edge of the shore. He raised his right arm. He stretched his staff out over the white waves. The waters trembled and divided. The wild wind roared. Soon a wall of water stood on the left and the right. Dry land appeared between the walls. A safe path to the other side! "Move, now!" Moses ordered. How strange it must have felt to step on to the sandy path. How scary to feel the spray from the water waiting on either side. Would God save them? Would God keep the promise to Moses?

In the morning, Pharaoh's army stood on the Red Sea's shore.

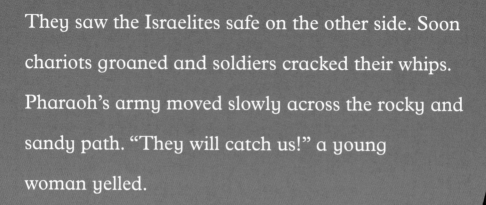

They saw the Israelites safe on the other side. Soon chariots groaned and soldiers cracked their whips. Pharaoh's army moved slowly across the rocky and sandy path. "They will catch us!" a young woman yelled.

"Watch and wait," said Moses. Moses once again held his staff up over the walls of waves.

Tons of water came tumbling down! Horses, chariots and riders were all swept into the sea.

From the safe shore came the sounds of singing and dancing, led by Miriam, Moses' sister. "Sing to the Lord," the Israelites shouted. "God has saved us!"

The Israelites were scared. Have you ever been scared? When? What did you do?

91

# Manna, Quail, and Water

God loved the Israelites and their leader, Moses. God promised to bring the people to a place where they could build homes and live happily. They had never lived outside of Egypt before, and they were afraid.

But God went with them as they walked long and far to the place God promised.

Traveling was hard and tiring. Along the way, the people became hungry. They complained to Moses. "I'm so hungry!" one boy cried. "I wish we could go back to Egypt!" whined a little girl. "At least we had food to eat there!" Her stomach growled. The people missed their dinners of meat and bread.

The Israelites didn't know that God heard them complaining. That evening, something strange happened. Tiny birds, called quails, appeared everywhere! God had sent the quails so the people could eat meat.

The next morning, the ground glistened with fresh dew. Even after the sun dried up the dew, there was still something covering the ground. It looked like bread had rained down from heaven! It was manna! The manna looked like tiny seeds and tasted like bread. The people ate and ate. Every day God sent manna and quails so that the people had food to eat.

The Israelites kept traveling toward the place God promised. After a while they ran out of water. Even though God had given them food when they were hungry, the people still complained. "My mouth feels dry like a desert!" sobbed a child. The people were thirsty.

This time God told Moses to hit a rock with his staff. When he did, water gushed out of the rock! The people had more than enough to drink. God gave food and water to the Israelites every day. God took care of the people, just like God promised.

What are some things you need that God provides for you?

# The Ten Commandments

The Israelites were on their way to the land God had promised them. It was a long way! With God watching over them, the men, women, and children walked and walked and walked over the hot, dry land. When they got tired and needed rest they would set up tents and camp together under the stars.

While they were camping at the bottom of a mountain called Mount Sinai something incredible happened. On the morning of the third day that they were there, a dark cloud covered the mountain. Crash! Boom! Bang! Lightning and thunder filled the sky. The people were afraid.

Suddenly, the voice of God called Moses.

God asked Moses to climb to the top of the mountain. So Moses grabbed his walking stick and climbed up, up, up.

97

When he got to the top of the mountain, God spoke. God said, "Moses, listen up! I have important rules for you and the people to live by. You can turn to this list to know how to love God and each other. Do your best to follow this list. It won't be easy, but I am with you and I love you."

Then, God gave Moses a list of 10 special rules called the commandments. They were:

**I am God, the only God. Honor me above all other things and people.**

**There are no other gods for you, only me.**

**My name is special. Don't use it with bad words or mean talk.**

Take a day of rest each week. Call it the Sabbath, and make it a special day for God.

Show your mom, dad, and others who take care of you love and respect.

Don't hurt others with your words or actions.

If you get married, you must be loyal to your husband or wife.

Don't take things that aren't yours.

Tell only the truth about your family, friends, and even those you do not know.

Be happy with what you have. Don't wish for things that other people have.

And with that, the dark cloud went away. Moses walked down, down, down the mountain. The people were still scared from the dark clouds and thunder. But Moses said, "Don't be afraid! God has given us special rules to teach us how to live together in peace." Moses told the people about God's rules, and they did their best to follow them.

Which of the Ten Commandments is the most difficult for you to follow? Why?

# The Battle of Jericho

The Israelites had finally gotten to the land God promised. They stood outside the tall, tall walls of the city called Jericho. God told Joshua that it was time for them to take over the city. So Joshua told the Israelites about God's plan.

"Here's what we will do," said Joshua. Joshua counted off seven

priests from the group—1, 2, 3, 4, 5, 6, 7. "You will each play a shofar. Keep blowing all the time, even if your lips get tired!" Next, Joshua looked at the soldiers in the group. "Grab your weapons and walk in front of the priests. The rest of you, walk behind the priests. Everyone needs to walk quietly. Any questions? Okay, let's go!"

The horns were loud! The people of Jericho could hear them through the thick stone walls of the city. What was happening?

The Israelites kept walking. Left, right, left went their marching feet around the city. The Israelites wondered how God's plan was going to work as they looked at the thick city walls.

The Israelites did this for six whole days. The people of Jericho watched every day. They had never seen anything like this before! Should they be afraid or should they laugh?

On the seventh day, the Israelites got up at sunrise and walked around the city seven times. After the seventh time, Joshua told the people to shout right after the priests blew the horns one last time. God's plan was for the walls to fall flat when the Israelites shouted.

The Israelites shouted so loud the ground began to shake! The thick, stone walls began to shake too, and soon they started to crumble! Huge stones crashed to the ground. The wall came tumbling down! The Israelites got what God promised.

Roll up a piece of paper to make a shofar and march around your room blowing it.

106

# Deborah

God's people had been captured by an enemy. They prayed to God, "Please help us get our land and freedom back!" God listened and sent a woman named Deborah to help them.

Deborah was a judge and was very wise and faithful to God. She gave people messages from God and helped people talk out their arguments. Every day, Deborah sat under a palm tree. Men and women who had problems came to her for help.

One day, God gave Deborah an important message—a message that would help free the people of Israel! Deborah gave God's message to a man named Barak. She told him, "God said, 'Take 10,000 men and go to Mount Tabor. God will help you defeat the king's army and the Israelites will be free!"

Barak said, "I'll do this, but I need your help!"
Deborah, who was as brave as she was wise, agreed to
go. She knew that God would be with her every step
along the way. Barak and Deborah took 10,000 men
to Mount Tabor. There was an awful battle! Yelling
and fighting went on—the noise was loud and terrible!
But God was always with Deborah and the Israelites,

protecting them and keeping them safe. It was a hard fight, but finally Barak and the Israelites won!

God helped them defeat the king's army, and there was peace for 40 years.

How do you think Deborah felt when she got messages from God to give to other people?

# Naomi and Ruth

Naomi lived together with her two daughters-in-law, Orpah and Ruth. They were the only people left in their household. Even when times were hard because a famine hit the land, the three were always happy together.

"Girls," Naomi said one day, "I've been thinking. Life is better where the rest of my family lives. Let's go there!"

So they packed all of their things and started off. Plod, plod, plod—it was a long and dusty walk! Halfway there, Naomi turned to Orpah and Ruth and said, "I am only your mother-in-law. You should go back and live with your mothers!" And with that, Naomi kissed them goodbye.

But Orpah and Ruth cried, "Boo hoo! We don't want to go back! We want to stay with you."

Naomi argued with them. "This doesn't make any sense! Go back without me, and start your lives over."

Dab, dab. Orpah dried the tears on her face and turned around on the dusty path, headed for home. But Ruth stayed with Naomi.

"I can't leave you!" Ruth said. "I will go where you go. I will live where you live. Your people will be my people, and your God will be my God." Ruth loved Naomi no matter what—just like God loves us no matter what!

Naomi saw that Ruth meant what she said. "All right," Naomi smiled, and they started walking again—plod, plod, plod. When Naomi's family saw her coming, they welcomed her with open arms. They shouted "Hooray!" and ran to hug her and Ruth.

"Welcome home!" they cried. Naomi and Ruth started their new life together, caring for each other, just as God cared for them.

Would you have acted more like Orpah or Ruth when Naomi said to turn back? Why?

# Ruth and Boaz

Ruth and Naomi were very, very poor. They didn't have any money to buy food to eat. Ruth said to Naomi, "I'm going to go to the field nearby to pick up some of the leftover grain so we can make some bread to eat. Hopefully, I'll meet someone who can help us."

In the field, Ruth walked behind the people who were harvesting the grain and picked up the leftovers for herself and Naomi. In the evenings she would grind

the grain into flour and use it to make bread so they could eat. Ruth was a very hard worker.

Ruth didn't know it, but she had picked a field that belonged to a rich man named Boaz. Boaz was also one of Naomi's relatives. When Boaz saw Ruth he asked, "Who is that young woman picking up the leftovers?"

The servant who was in charge of all the workers in the field said, "Oh, her? She isn't from here. She came with Naomi and asked if she could have some of the leftovers. She is a hard worker!"

When Boaz met Ruth, he told her she could stay in his field and work with the other women. "If you get tired or thirsty," he said, "please stop and rest and have a drink of water."

Ruth was very grateful. "Why are you being so nice to me?" she asked shyly.

Boaz said, "I've heard how hard you work and how kind you have been to Naomi. I think God must be very proud of you and I would like to help you."

Boaz told his workers to be very kind to Ruth and to let her take all the grain that she wanted for herself and Naomi.

Pretend you are Ruth picking up leftover grain out of the field as you pick up your toys. Is it hard or easy work? What if you did it all day long?

117

# Hannah Prays for a Child

Hannah dreamed of having a baby to love and hold. She dreamed of singing lullabies to him until he fell asleep in her arms. But year after year passed and Hannah had no baby. Her friends laughed at her and called her names. Hannah cried and cried! Even though she was sad, Hannah prayed in the temple every day. She prayed, "Oh God, if you give me a son, I will make sure that he spends his life serving you!"

Eli, the priest at the temple, watched Hannah as she prayed. Her lips moved quickly, but she didn't make a sound. He thought this was very strange, so he said to her, "Stop acting so silly!"

"Oh no, sir!" Hannah said. "I'm not acting silly. I'm praying to God because I want to have a baby."

Eli looked into her eyes and said to her, "Go in peace. God will give you what you're asking for."

Hannah trusted in God. Soon, her tears turned into joy. God gave her a son, and she named him Samuel. Hannah was so happy! She laughed and danced and kissed Samuel all over his little face. She sang lullabies to Samuel and held him close as he fell asleep.

Soon it was time for Hannah to keep the promise she had made to God. When Samuel was still a boy, she took him to Eli at the temple.

She said, "I'm the woman who was here praying to God for a baby. God gave me a son, Samuel. Now he will spend his life serving God." Samuel stayed at the temple with Eli. He grew and grew and grew, serving God every day of his life.

Do you know someone who is having a hard time? Pray for them and tell them God loves them.

# God Calls Samuel

Samuel was a 12-year-old boy who lived in the temple with a priest named Eli and learned about God. Eli took care of Samuel, and Samuel helped take care of Eli because Eli was almost blind. One night something special happened.

As Samuel slept in the temple he heard a voice call out, "Samuel." Samuel thought it was Eli calling, so he jumped up from his bed. "Here I am," Samuel answered as he ran to Eli. "I'm here because you called me."

But Eli shook his head. "I didn't call you. Go back to your bed."

Samuel did as he was told and fell asleep quickly.
A little while later the voice called again, "Samuel."
This time Samuel was more tired and crawled out
of his bed more slowly. In Eli's room, Samuel rubbed
his eyes, scratched his tummy, and said with a yawn,
"I'm here because you called me."

Eli was getting tired of Samuel coming into his
room and said more firmly, "I didn't call you!
Now please go back to bed!"

When this happened a third time Eli thought to himself, "Aha! It must be God who is calling Samuel!" Eli told Samuel, who was now very confused and sleepy, "If you are called again, just say, 'God, I hear you and I will do whatever you want.'" When the voice called again Samuel did as Eli told him. It was God! And God had many things to say to Samuel.

Even though he was only 12, Samuel wanted to serve God. With God's help, Samuel grew up to share many messages from God. People all over Israel knew Samuel as God's trusted prophet.

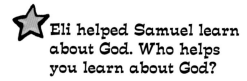

Eli helped Samuel learn about God. Who helps you learn about God?

# David Is Chosen

God said to Samuel, "I have a job for you. I want you to anoint a new king. Here's what you need to do. Bring a horn filled with oil to Bethlehem and look for Jesse and all his sons. One of his sons will be the next king." Samuel was afraid that God's job was too scary. The old king was still around and he was a very mean guy. But God promised Samuel, "I'll help you."

So Samuel walked to Bethlehem and found Jesse. "Line up all your sons and let's see who will be the next king," Samuel said to Jesse.

Samuel looked at the first son, Eliab, and felt sure God

would choose him to be king. Eliab was big and good looking. But God disagreed. Samuel was looking at the outside of Eliab, seeing how strong he looked. God was looking on the inside and did not see the right love in Eliab's heart.

One by one the sons came forward to see if they would be chosen.

This one? Nope, sorry. This one? Uh, no. How about this one? Don't think so.

Finally they ran out of sons. Except for one, that is! Jesse's son David was outside watching the sheep. They called for him.

David came inside. He smelled a little bit like sheep, but his eyes sparkled with joy and love.

David was just a boy, gentle and quiet. Samuel tried to see David from outside and inside.

This one? A hush fell over the room as everyone waited.

"Yes!" God told Samuel. "Yes!" Samuel told everyone. Samuel poured oil from the horn onto David's head, anointing him with God's love and joy. David would be the next king!

Using cooking oil, draw a cross on the foreheads of your family members to anoint them!

# David
# and Goliath

King Saul and his army looked out from their
mountain hideout. Their enemies, the Philistines, were
camped on the opposite mountain. In the valley between
stood Goliath, the tallest man Saul had ever seen.

"Who will fight me?" Goliath roared, waving his
spear. "Who can face the mighty Goliath?" he shouted,
lifting his sword.

Saul and his army were afraid. They could not win against the Philistines. They could not beat Goliath. Surely they would be captured and become slaves.

A beam of sunlight bounced off of Goliath's bronze helmet. His voice shook the leaves in the trees. All the birds hid behind their branches.

"Send out your best warrior," Goliath ordered. "Let him fight against me. If I win, you will be our slaves. If your soldier wins, we will serve you and your God."

Saul waited. No one stepped forward to take Goliath's challenge. Saul felt a small tug on his sleeve. Looking down, he saw David, a young shepherd boy.

"I will do it, King Saul," David said. "I will fight Goliath."

"You are a boy. How can you beat a gigantic man like Goliath?" Saul turned to go.

"Wait, King Saul," David said. "God protects me from the wolves and bears that go after my sheep. God will protect me now too."

David reached down and picked up five smooth stones. In his right hand he carried the same sling he used to chase away the wolves and wild animals. Saul patted David's head and pointed down the rocky path leading to the valley.

Goliath laughed when he saw David. "You are the warrior they send out against me?"

David slipped his hand into his pouch and selected a stone. "I am not afraid of your spear and sword, Goliath," David said.

"God will help me." David rushed toward Goliath, swinging his sling. The smooth stone flew through the air and hit Goliath in the forehead.

133

Down, down, down Goliath fell. Down fell his sword. Down fell his spear. Down fell his mighty shield. David picked up Goliath's bronze helmet from the ground and held it high in the air. Saul and all his soldiers rose up with a shout! David, a small shepherd boy, had beaten the mighty Goliath.

When the Philistines saw that Goliath had fallen, they were afraid and ran away. Trusting in God gave David courage when he needed it most.

Keep a small, smooth stone in your pocket. Touch it whenever you feel afraid. Remember that God is with you.

# Solomon Builds the Temple

David was a great king for God's people. God told David that his son, Solomon, would build a temple. When Solomon became the king, he wanted to build a temple so God could live there. He wanted the temple to be the most dazzling, amazing building ever built. Solomon decided he would build the temple out of beautiful and expensive materials.

First, Solomon told his workers to dig large stones out of the ground. "I don't want God to hear any loud building noises here," Solomon told the workers. "You need to measure, cut, and shape the stones out in the hills before you bring them here." The workers did what Solomon told them to do.

Next, Solomon told his workers to make the roof and the floor out of a hard, sturdy wood called cedar.

137

"Carve designs of flowers into the cedar wood and decorate the temple with the carvings," Solomon directed. "The nice smell and elegant designs will make God happy." The workers did what Solomon told them to do.

Finally, Solomon made a room especially for God. "Cover the entire room in gold," he said. The workers did what Solomon told them to do. The room glowed and shimmered.

When the temple was finished, Solomon put a special box called the Ark of the Covenant into the room of gold. The people had put God's Ten Commandments in the box. Wherever the Ark of the Covenant was, God was there too.

The people went to the temple every day to worship God. The temple was the most impressive building ever built for God, and God was happy to live in the temple Solomon built!

★ The people worshipped God in the temple to feel close to God. Where do you feel close to God?

139

# Elijah and the Widow

Elijah was a prophet. God helped him show and tell others about God. One day God said, "Pack your things, Elijah. It's time to move to a new town. I have told a widow there to feed you. I will make a miracle."

It was not a good time to move. Rain had not fallen for many days. The sun was hot and the earth was dry. Elijah didn't have any friends in the new town. But he listened to God and went to the new town.

When Elijah finally got to the town he was thirsty. Just then, he spotted a woman. Could this be the widow God told him about? "Excuse me, ma'am? Could you please bring me a drink of water?" The kind woman hurried to get the water.

"Grrr!" Elijah's tummy growled. He remembered that God said the widow would feed him. He called after her, "Excuse me, ma'am? Could you please bring me a nibble of bread to eat?" The woman stopped in her tracks. She turned to face Elijah.

The widow had sad eyes. "I'm sorry, sir. I don't have any bread," she sighed. "The last of my oil and flour will only make a biscuit. My son and I are going to split it as our last meal. We have no other food." She started to cry.

"Dry your tears," Elijah said. "God will make a miracle for you. Bake the bread and share it with me. God promises that your flour and oil will not run out."

The widow mixed, kneaded, and baked loaf after loaf of bread. Her jar of flour and jug of oil made plenty of food for Elijah, herself, and her son. God's promise was kept. It was a miracle!

You can help feed others too! Gather extra canned food from your house and give it to a food bank.

# Elisha Feeds 100

The prophet Elisha worked for God. He gave the people messages from God. Elisha prayed for people and helped them give their offerings to God.

A man went to see Elisha. "I hope Elisha will help me," the man thought. He was carrying a special bag. The bag was special because he used it to carry his offering to God. Inside the bag were 20 loaves of bread. The bread was made with the first grains of barley that were grown in the man's field. The man walked up to Elisha and gave Elisha the bag. "This is my offering for God," the man said.

Elisha peeked inside the bag. When he saw what was inside, Elisha said a surprising thing. "Take this bread and give it to the people to eat." The man looked confused. He thought he was bringing his bread for God. "Give it to the people?" he asked. "There are 100 people waiting to eat! How can 20 loaves of bread feed 100 people?"

Elisha repeated what he had said a bit louder.

"Take this bread and give it to the people to eat!"

The man still did not understand. He frowned at Elisha

and shook his head. When Elisha saw the look on the

man's face, he reminded the man of God's promise.

"God promised to take care of us. God will give us

enough food to eat. We will even have leftovers!"

The man finally listened to Elisha. Carefully, he opened the bag and gave the people the bread. He waited. Would there be enough? Could all 100 people eat? Yes! All 100 people ate bread until they were full! When they were through, the man helped clean up. Then he noticed a wonderful thing: there were leftovers, just as Elisha had said!

How much food do you think it would take to feed 100 people dinner at your house?

# Naaman Is Healed

Naaman was in charge of a very big army for the king of a place called Aram. He was a big, strong, and important man in his country. Sadly, Naaman had a disease called leprosy, which gave him painful sores on his body that would not go away.

A young Israelite girl was a servant in Naaman's household and knew of a prophet named Elisha in her country who could heal Naaman's leprosy.

When Naaman heard this, he asked the king if he could go to Israel to be healed. The king liked Naaman, so he told him he could go.

Elisha heard that Naaman was coming. So Elisha sent his messenger to Naaman and told him to go wash seven times in the river to heal his leprosy.

Naaman was angry! "Why didn't the prophet Elisha come here and heal me? I am an important man!" he fumed. "I could wash in the rivers in my own country! What's so special about this little river?" he demanded.

149

"At least try!" Naaman's servant exclaimed. "We've come a long way."

"All right," Naaman muttered. He went to the edge of the river and stuck his big toe in. Nothing happened.

"All the way in," ordered Naaman's servant.

Naaman went all the way in and came out dripping wet. He counted with his big booming voice every time he went into the water. "1 . . . 2 . . . 3 . . . 4 . . . 5 . . . 6 . . . 7!" Naaman washed himself in the river seven times, just like Elisha said to do.

After the seventh time, Naaman looked down at his skin. It worked! Naaman was shocked. Now he knew that God was amazing. He went home praising and thanking God.

⭐ During bath time, dunk in the water seven times. Talk about what you would do or say if God healed you.

# Queen Esther

Once there was a girl named Esther. When she was young, Esther was adopted by her cousin Mordecai. She grew into a lovely young woman. One day, the king decreed that he needed a new queen. Esther and other young women from the kingdom were presented to the king. When the king saw Esther he said, "You are the one. I want you to be my queen!"

Esther and Mordecai were Jewish, but the people who worshipped other gods did not like the Jewish people. Esther had not told the king or anyone else in the palace that she and Mordecai were Jewish. One of those who hated Jewish people was the one of the king's top officials, Haman. The king said, "Because Haman is so important, everyone should kneel and bow down to him!" This made Haman happy because he thought a lot of himself.

But Mordecai knew he should only bow down to God. When Haman saw that Mordecai wouldn't bow down to him, he was mad. And when he learned Mordecai was Jewish, he was even madder!

Haman said. "I am going to use my power to have Mordecai and all of the Jewish people killed."

Mordecai was scared. He asked Esther to tell the king to stop Haman. "Maybe this is the reason you have become queen," he said, "Perhaps God knew that we would need you to save us."

Esther was afraid. If she told the king she was Jewish, she could be killed too! But if she didn't tell him, all of her people would be killed. She decided to risk her life to try and save her people.

"I have found out something important," Esther said. "Haman is planning to kill all of the Jewish people!" And then Esther told him her secret. She was Jewish too.

The king loved Esther. He stopped Haman's plan. Haman was taken away and the king gave Haman's job to Mordecai.

"Here is my ring for you to wear," the king said to Mordecai. "Write a message to all of the Jewish people in my kingdom. Tell them they are safe. Use my name and seal the letters with my ring."

The letters went to people all across the land, and they celebrated with music, feasting, and dancing.

"Hurray for Queen Esther!" the people cheered. "Because of her bravery, we are saved!"

What would you have done if you were Esther in this story? Why?

157

# The Lord Is My Shepherd

David, the shepherd, loved his sheep. He led them to beautiful fields where they ran, played, jumped, and kicked up their heels. They ate the lush green grass and feasted on delicious berries. They drank from cool mountain streams and splashed in refreshing waterfalls.

David cared for each and every lamb. If one wandered over the hill, David was quick to go and find it. He put the lost lamb on his shoulders and sang sweet songs and hummed soft melodies. Sometimes he played his harp to help the tired lambs fall asleep.

During times of danger, David fought against wild animals with only a slingshot and some stones. His sheep were not afraid because David was always with them.

David thought about what he did as a shepherd, and thought that God cares for people in many of the same ways that he cared for his sheep. One day, David wrote a song to tell everyone God is like a shepherd. God loves and cares for each and every one of us.

God is my shepherd, he gives me all I need.
He gives me wonderful places to rest and sleep.
He lets me splash and play in cool, clear waters.
He helps me do what is right.
I am not afraid even in the darkest nights
Because you are with me, God, and
Your protection comforts me.
When danger comes, you give me strength.
My life is filled with your love, and all I want is to be
With you my whole life long.

David sang his song to his sheep, thankful for

all the ways God loved and cared for him.

**How do you know that God loves and protects you all the time?**

# A Child Called Immanuel

King Ahaz, the king of Judah, would not listen to God. He wanted to become friends with people from another country who didn't believe in God. God knew this was a bad idea, because the people in the other country really wanted to hurt King Ahaz and his people. God warned. God pleaded. King Ahaz would not change his mind. He wanted his own way.

"Ask me for a sign," God said. "Then you will know that I am your God. Then you will listen to me."

God sent a prophet, Isaiah, to talk with King Ahaz. Isaiah did what God asked him to do. His job was to be God's voice. Isaiah warned King Ahaz that bad things would happen to him and his people if he did not listen to God. Isaiah promised that God would protect King Ahaz and his country if he listened. God even gave King Ahaz a sign to look for—a child to show him the way.

Isaiah said a child would be born and live with the people. His name would be Immanuel. Immanuel means "God with us." Then the people would know how much God loved them and they would listen to God.

King Ahaz crossed his arms and shook his head. Who was Isaiah to tell him what to do?

"I am the king!" King Ahaz said.

"People listen to me. Why should I listen to you or your God, Isaiah?"

King Ahaz did not listen to God and soon things went very bad for King Ahaz. His crops dried up. There was very little food. Soon his country was taken over by others.

Other people, the Israelites, did listen to Isaiah. They remembered God's promise and waited many years for God's sign, Immanuel, to be born.

**Think of a time when you did not listen to someone. What happened?**

# God's Peaceful World

The people of Israel had been at war for a long time. They were tired and weary. They needed a leader who would help them. God promised to send them a leader. The leader would be a strong and wise child who would show them how to live in peace.

God promised that the child would come from King David's family and that he would be an ancestor of Jesse, King David's father.

God promised to lead the child. "I will always be with him," God said.

God promised to make the child wise. "A good leader must know all kinds of things. He must be able to make good decisions. The child will be very smart and teach others too," God said.

167

"I love you more than all of creation," God told the people. "I want you to love me too. The child will know and love me. He will show you how to love me."

God knew the child could bring peace to the world. He would be a wise judge who would bring justice to the poor. "I love all people. I want you to learn to love all people. Whether the people are rich or poor, I want you to love them. Whether they are hungry or full, love them. Whether their skin is the color of chocolate, snow, butterscotch, roses, or anything in between, love them. Then you can live in peace."

God promised that when the child came, wolves and lambs would live together in peace. So would leopards and baby goats, as well as lions and calves.

If animals who are natural enemies can live together in peace, then people can too. The child would show them how to live in peace and love each other.

Pretend to be like an animal in the story: maybe a wolf, lamb, lion, calf.

# Fiery Furnace

King Nebuchadnezzar was so angry that his face got all scrunched up and almost turned purple. Why was he so mad? Shadrach, Meshach, and Abednego, three of his workers, had said "No!" when King Nebuchadnezzar declared that everyone had to bow down to a huge golden statue he had made of himself.

Shadrach, Meshach, and Abednego knew that God was the only one they should worship. But this made King Nebuchadnezzar so angry! No one disobeyed the king!

The king demanded to have the men tied up and thrown into the furnace. He even ordered to have the furnace turned up seven times hotter than normal. Ouch! It was hot! When King Nebuchadnezzar peeked into the furnace to see Shadrach, Meshach, and Abednego, he was surprised.

"I thought we threw three men in there," he shouted. "But I see four men walking around in there, and they aren't even tied up! They're fine! What's going on?"

The extra man in the furnace was an angel sent by God to protect the three men from the fire.

The king flung open the door of the hot, fiery furnace and called, "Shadrach, Meshach, and Abednego, come out right now!"

When they came out everyone noticed that the fire hadn't hurt them. They didn't even smell like smoke! King Nebuchadnezzar was amazed, realizing what had happened. "Your God sent an angel to protect you. You disobeyed me and faced death rather than worship someone other than God. I declare that no one in any country can say anything against the God of Shadrach, Meshach, and Abednego because no god can do what their God can do."

When do you get scared? How do you know God is with you at scary times?

173

# Daniel and the Lions

Daniel loved God. He prayed every day and tried to live as God told him to. Daniel knew that no matter what God was always with him. Daniel's good friend, King Darius, put Daniel in charge of many things in his kingdom. Some men got very jealous of Daniel and decided to get him in trouble. "Heh! Heh!" they thought. "We'll get Daniel yet!"

The men tricked the king into making a law that everyone had to pray to King Darius and not God! Anyone who broke this law would be placed into a den full of lions—YIKES!

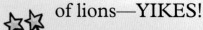

Daniel was very afraid of lions, but he prayed to God anyway! Daniel knew he could get into big trouble. He also knew God would always be with him.

Trouble came quickly. The men who tricked King Darius saw Daniel praying. "Aha!" they said. "We've got him! Now he won't be the king's favorite!" They went to tell the king. "King Darius! Daniel is praying to his God instead of you!" King Darius looked puzzled. Daniel always prayed to his God. What was the big deal? Then the men reminded him. "You must put Daniel into the lions' den! You made it a law, remember?"

Oh no! King Darius didn't want to put Daniel in the lions' den! He didn't want Daniel to be hurt! But King Darius had to follow his own law. Daniel was put in with the lions. King Darius said, "I hope your God helps you!" He went home and stayed awake

all night worrying

about Daniel.

In the lions' den, it was dark and scary.
Lions growled all around Daniel.
Daniel prayed, "God, I know you
are with me. Please help me!"

God was with Daniel.

At sunrise, King Darius hurried to the lions' den and had it opened. "Daniel?" he called. "Are you there? Did your God save you?" Daniel answered, "I'm here! God kept the lions from hurting me! God always keeps me safe!" King Darius was overjoyed to see his friend. From that day on King Darius believed in God.

How do you know that God is always with you, even in hard times?

179

# Jonah and the Big Fish

One day, when Jonah was just minding his own business, God spoke to him. God said, "Jonah, I want you to go to Nineveh and tell the people that I know they aren't living the way I want them to! I want them to change their ways."

Jonah may have started with the right idea, but once he started walking, Jonah began thinking about what a long walk it was to Nineveh. "Hmmm," Jonah thought, "I don't really want to go to Nineveh—I'll go the other way! God will never know." So Jonah walked and walked—away from Nineveh. When Jonah got to the sea, he paid to get onto a boat to take him even farther away.

"Aahhhhh," Jonah yawned. "All that walking made me tired! I'm going to take a nap."

Jonah curled
up on a pile of
rope and fell
asleep.

But God
saw Jonah!
WHOOSH!
God sent a
strong wind
that tossed the ship
to and fro. The sailors
were so afraid that they started
throwing things overboard to make the
boat lighter and save themselves.

The sailors worried.

 "What's going on?"

They woke Jonah up.

"God is mad at me for not listening," Jonah said, "so throw *me* overboard!" And they did! Suddenly the sea was calm again.

Look out, Jonah! Here comes a BIG fish! Gulp, gulp, gulp. The fish swallowed Jonah, and Jonah sat inside the dark, smelly fish for three days and three nights. Jonah prayed, "Help me God! I'm sorry." Finally, the fish spit Jonah out on the beach.

Trudge, trudge, trudge. Jonah went to Nineveh. He told the people what God had said, and they believed him and changed the way they were living. God was happy that the people of Nineveh were now living as God wanted.

 **Pretend you're on a boat. The winds are blowing. Waves are rocking the boat. Now you know how Jonah felt.**

# A Ruler from Bethlehem

Micah was a prophet. He spoke to the people for God. During the time when Micah was alive, God's people were afraid. They felt sad and hopeless. God sent Micah to the people of Bethlehem, one of the smallest groups of God's people, with some unbelievable news.

This is the good news that Micah announced to God's people.

"From you, little Bethlehem, will come a wonderful leader for the whole world! He will be like a good shepherd who loves and takes care of each sheep in his flock. He will take care of *all* people—especially those who need extra help. *All* God's people will be safe with this leader because he will lead with peace and fairness. He will be the greatest leader the world has ever seen. There is hope! Live with hope, you people of Bethlehem!"

Find one person whom you can care for today! Tell that person why you care.

# Angels Visit

Mary was a young woman. She lived in a town called Nazareth and was engaged to be married to a man named Joseph. One day, a tall and handsome man appeared in front of Mary. His clothes were brilliant white. His hair was dark and curly, and his eyes sparkled like lights. Mary knew the man must be an angel.

"Hello, Mary," he said. "God is with you." Mary stepped backward. His deep voice scared her.

"Don't be afraid," he said. "God sent me to tell you that you are going to have a son, who you'll name Jesus. He is going to be very important to many people."

"A son? But I'm not married yet," she said. "How is this going to happen?"

"The Holy Spirit will come to you," the angel replied. "Your son will be the Son of God."

*The Son of God? My son?* Mary thought about all these things. It didn't seem possible, but she believed anything was possible for God. "I am God's servant,

I'll do whatever God says," she said, but her mind was racing. *What will Joseph think? Would he believe her?* Mary was nervous.

When Mary told Joseph about the angel and about giving birth to God's Son, he did just what she was afraid he would do. He didn't believe her. He talked about not marrying her anymore. Mary felt so sad. But she remembered what the angel said and she trusted God.

The next day, something wonderful happened. Joseph came to her and said, "An angel came to me in a dream! He said, 'Joseph, don't be afraid to make Mary your wife. She is going to have a son and you're going to name him Jesus. He's going to save people from their sins.'"

Mary smiled a big smile. She was so happy that tears of joy filled her eyes and trickled down her cheeks. She felt Joseph's love again.

"I am not scared for you to be my wife, Mary," he said. "I will be with you and we will name the boy Jesus."

**Make up a dance that Mary might have done after she heard the good news.**

191

# Mary Visits Elizabeth

One day Mary hurried to visit her cousin Elizabeth. She had an exciting surprise to share! Elizabeth was going to have a baby, and Mary wanted to tell her that she was going to have a baby too.

"Hello, Elizabeth!" Mary called when she arrived at the house. "Are you surprised to see me?"

Elizabeth stared at Mary with big, wide eyes. She was so excited to see Mary that she didn't know what to say. The sound of Mary's voice even made the baby inside Elizabeth wiggle and squirm for joy! Without even asking, Elizabeth knew the secret Mary wanted to tell her.

With tears in her eyes she hugged Mary warmly and said, "Mary, God has blessed you more than any other woman, and God has blessed the baby you will have! Can you guess how I know? As soon as you said hello to me my own baby wiggled with happiness inside of me. Because you believe God keeps promises, you have been blessed."

Mary was so full of joy that her words sounded like a beautiful song. "I praise God and I am so happy because of God my Savior. God has chosen me, a simple servant. From now on, all people will know that God has blessed me. God has done something wonderful for me, and God's name is holy.

God shows kindness to people who obey God, gives power to the poor, and feeds hungry people. God has helped the people of Israel by keeping the promises made to our ancestor Abraham and his family forever."

Mary stayed with Elizabeth for three months. They had so much fun getting ready for their babies and talking about what their children might be like when they grew up. When the time came for Mary to leave, she felt sad. She said to Elizabeth, "God be with you and your baby until we see each other again." Elizabeth said, "God be with you and your baby too, Mary."

Soon it was time for Elizabeth to have her baby. She gave birth to a baby boy, a son. Elizabeth's family and friends were very happy for her! God was so good to Elizabeth.

When you have exciting news to share, how do you tell your family and friends?

197

# Jesus Is Born

"We have to go to Bethlehem," Joseph told Mary. "Emperor Augustus has ordered that all of the people need to be counted."

"But Joseph," Mary said, "what about our baby? He will be born soon."

"We'll go slowly, Mary. Bethlehem will be crowded so we need to leave now."

So Mary and Joseph journeyed to Bethlehem, the City of David, to be counted along with all of the other people. It was cold when they arrived. Joseph knocked on many doors looking for a room, but everyone said no. Finally, an innkeeper answered his door.

"I have no room," the innkeeper said. "But you can stay in the little stable in the back. It's warm, and the hay is fresh."

"Joseph," Mary said. "I think it's time for the baby to be born."

That night Mary gave birth to Jesus. She laid him in a manger. The animals kept them warm as they waited for morning.

Outside of Bethlehem, shepherds watched their sheep on the hills. Suddenly, an angel appeared. The shepherds looked up at the bright night sky.

"Don't be afraid," the angel said. "I bring wonderful news. The child God promised was born tonight." The shepherds listened in amazement. The twinkling stars seemed to echo each of the angel's words.

The angel continued, "Go to Bethlehem! You will find the child lying in a bed of hay!"

Suddenly, many angels filled the heavens. They sang together, *"Glory to God in the highest. And peace to all people on earth."*

"Let's hurry!" one shepherd said. "The angel said the child was born tonight!"

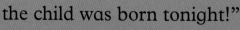

"But what about the sheep?" another shepherd asked.

"Let the angels watch them!"

the youngest shepherd said.

"Yes! Let the angels watch them!" The shepherds

happily hurried into Bethlehem.

201

The angel was right. The shepherds found the baby, Jesus, asleep on a bed of hay. They told Mary and Joseph all the angel had said.

"The angel said the baby is the Messiah—the promised one. He is the one we have waited for," they explained. "But this is a stable. Would God be born here among the animals?"

"Moo-o-o-o," said the cow.

"Baa-a-a-a," said the sheep.

"Coo-o-o-o," said the dove.

Mary smiled. She knew that Jesus was

Immanuel—God with us.

Later the shepherds returned to their sheep, praising

God for all they had seen and heard. Jesus was born!

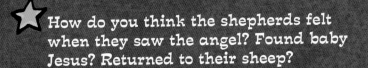

How do you think the shepherds felt when they saw the angel? Found baby Jesus? Returned to their sheep?

# Wise Men

On a cool, clear evening, three wise men looked into the night sky and saw a bright star. The wise men had been waiting for someone important to come into the world. They were waiting for a king. They knew that the star was a sign from God.

"The star is a sign that the king has been born!" the shortest one said.

"We should follow the star and find him!" the tallest one said.

"I'll pack our bags!" the middle one said.

They left their homes and traveled far to meet this new baby king. They wanted to worship him and give him gifts.

205

Along the way, they stopped and visited King Herod, the ruler of the that land. "We are following the star to find the baby king," they told King Herod. "Do you know where he is?"

When King Herod heard that the baby king had been born, he was afraid. He thought the baby would grow up and take over. Then Herod wouldn't be the king anymore. So King Herod spoke to the wise men. He pretended to be nice. Herod told the wise men, "I would like to meet the new baby king. Why don't you go find him and come back here and tell me where he is? Then I can go worship him too."

The wise men kept following the star to find the baby. They finally found Jesus, Mary, and Joseph in Bethlehem. They were quiet so they wouldn't wake baby Jesus. They knelt beside his bed. He was so tiny!

They kissed his little cheek. "Sleep well, little one," they said, and they left him gifts of gold, frankincense, and myrrh. Those were very expensive gifts. They were gifts fit for a king.

Later, the wise men decided it was time to go home. They were planning to tell King Herod where they found baby Jesus, but God sent an angel to talk to them in a dream. The angel told them that King Herod was dangerous. So they went home a different way instead.

Jesus was, indeed, a new baby king who surprised the wise men and frightened King Herod. Jesus was God's promise born for us, a gift to all people.

Make a gift for someone special.
Draw a picture, make a clay sculpture,
or string buttons into a necklace.

# Simeon and Anna

There was an old man named Simeon who lived in Jerusalem. Simeon loved God. He knew God's words and believed God's promises. God made a promise to Simeon. God promised Simeon that he would not die until he saw the person God was sending to save the whole world!

One day Simeon went to the temple. The temple was very crowded. Many people were there. Mary, Joseph, and baby Jesus were there too. Simeon looked around. When Simeon saw baby Jesus he got very excited! Could Jesus be the one? Simeon pointed at baby Jesus and asked, "May I hold him?" "Carefully," Mary said. Simeon carefully picked Jesus up and began praising God!

211

Simeon said, "God, you have kept your promise! You have let me see the one you promised to send. He will save the whole world!"

Mary and Joseph were amazed! Was Jesus part of God's promise to save the whole world? "What does this mean?" Joseph asked. "How can this be?" Simeon talked about God's promise with Mary and Joseph. Then he blessed Jesus and his family.

An old woman named Anna was also at the temple. Anna lived at the temple. She worshipped God and prayed day and night. When Anna saw Jesus, she rushed over. She knew Jesus was special. Would Mary let Anna hold Jesus too? "Yes," Mary said. Anna began praising God too! She told everyone who would listen, "Jesus is the one God promised to send. Jesus will save the world!" Then Anna handed Jesus back to Joseph. "Take good care of him," Anna said. "Oh, we will," Joseph said.

What an exciting day! When Mary and Joseph finished at the temple, they took Jesus home to Nazareth. Jesus grew up in Nazareth. He became strong and wise, and God was always with him.

If you were thanking God for Jesus, what would you say?

# The Boy at the Temple

Every year Jesus' family traveled from their home
in Nazareth to Jerusalem to celebrate the festival of
Passover. Jesus loved going to

the festival. He loved the crowds of people. He loved the noise and bustle of activity. And he loved spending time in the temple.

One year, when Jesus was 12, the festival began like any other. Joseph, Mary, and Jesus enjoyed the sights, sounds, and activities of the festival together. When the festival was over, Mary and Joseph joined others from Nazareth for the long walk home. But when the group stopped to camp at the end of the first day, Mary and Joseph could not find Jesus anywhere!

Everyone thought he had been walking with someone else in the group. "Jeeeeeeesuuuuusss!" yelled his parents. "Jesus, where are you?"

Mary and Joseph were frantic! They quickly walked back to Jerusalem looking for him. They searched the city high and low for three whole days until they found Jesus in the temple. Mary and Joseph were surprised at what they saw. Jesus was in the temple, talking with teachers more than twice his age! He was just a boy, but he could talk about God with a room full of grown-ups! The teachers in the temple were impressed with what Jesus knew. Mary and Joseph were proud, but they were still a bit angry with Jesus. "Jesus, why weren't you with us? We have been looking all over for you," Mary and Joseph exclaimed.

Jesus replied, "Why were you looking for me? Didn't you understand that I was in my Father's house?"

Mary and Joseph didn't understand, but with that, they gathered their belongings and began the long walk back home.

⭐ **What do you think Jesus meant when he said, "I was in my Father's house"?**

# John the Baptist

John was an unusual man. He had lots of hair and a long beard. His clothes looked like his face—they, too, were furry and hairy! His clothes were made of camel's hair, held together with a leather belt! John ate strange foods, including wild honey and locusts, a kind of grasshopper. YUCK!

God gave John an important job. His job was to tell people that Jesus was coming and help them get ready to believe what Jesus would teach them. John knew the things Jesus would tell people were the most important things in the world.

When he taught people, John stood by the river and yelled out, "Hey! All of you! Tell God you're sorry for your sins! Turn your life around and act in ways that are good and honest!"

Then he would turn to another group and shout, "Are you listening?!? This is important! Jesus is coming!

He is the Messiah! He will save all of us!" Day after day, John continued teaching, preaching, and crying out so people would listen.

Many people came to hear what John had to say about Jesus. There were rich and poor people, honest and dishonest people, nice and not-so-nice people.

221

Some people listened to John. Some people didn't.
Some people said, "That man must be a messenger
from God!" Some said, "He is really odd! I'm getting
out of here!"

Many people believed the message John told. Those people said, "I am sorry for my sins. I want God to forgive me!" To each, John said, "God does forgive you!" He baptized those people in the river. The people started calling him John the Baptist. John the Baptist had done a good job. The people were ready to hear the message Jesus would bring!

What things about Jesus can you tell someone? Say them loudly to a friend or family member.

# Jesus' Baptism

While Jesus was living in Galilee, his cousin, John the Baptist, was preaching out in the country of Judea. The people loved John and came to see and hear him whenever they could.

Sometimes crowds of people came to see John by the Jordan River. When the crowds came John would tell them, "Change what needs changing in your life! God's kingdom is here!" The people would promise to change their lives, and then John would baptize them to show that they were a new person in God's eyes.

"I baptize you on the outside with plain old water from the Jordan River, but this is nothing compared to what and who is coming!" John would exclaim. "The one who is coming will baptize you with God's own Spirit! With God's Spirit, you will be changed from the inside out!"

While John was saying this, Jesus appeared.
He asked John to baptize him. But John wasn't so sure.

"What? Me baptize YOU? I think it should be the
other way around!" John said.

But Jesus insisted. "Do it, John! God does amazing
things in baptism!"

So John did what Jesus asked and baptized him.
All the way under the water in the Jordan River Jesus
went. When he splashed up out of the river, Jesus saw
the skies open up and he saw God's Spirit! It looked
like a dove gracefully floating down to land on him.

There was a voice too. The voice said, "This is my Son! He has been chosen and marked by my love! He is the great joy of my life!"

How are you a great joy of God's life?

# Jesus Goes to Nazareth

Jesus went to synagogues, holy places where people worshipped, to teach people about God. He went to synagogues all over—even in his hometown, Nazareth. Jesus told the people, "I was sent to tell you that God loves you and poor people and sick people and people in prison." But the people didn't believe Jesus' words.

"Why are you talking about sick people and poor people and people in prison?

Everyone knows that God doesn't care about them," they said.

"I am here to show you that God's way is love for all people!" said Jesus.

The people began to grumble. Their grumbling grew to shouting. Their shouting turned to shoving. Their shoving turned to chasing Jesus out of the synagogue.

"Go away Jesus!" Jesus went away from there, but he kept on telling people and showing people about God's love.

Think of someone who is sick. Pray for that person to know God loves him or her.

# Jesus Heals

Jesus enjoyed teaching and healing. People everywhere heard that Jesus was a healer. They brought their sick family and friends to Jesus so he could heal them. When Jesus was near sick people, he could have gotten sick too. But Jesus didn't get sick. Instead, Jesus healed the people. He went out of his way to help.

Early one morning, Jesus went to his friend Simon Peter's house. Simon Peter was very upset. "Jesus, my wife's mother has a terrible fever. I know you have healed people in many places. Would you please heal her too?"

Jesus could feel how sad his friend was. He knelt down next to the woman, held her hand, and healed her.

Jesus and his friends kept going from town to town healing others and teaching people about God's love.

If you could bring someone to Jesus to be healed, who would you bring? Why?

# The Disciples

Jesus told everyone he met, "Repent! Stop the bad things you are doing and start doing good!" One day Jesus was at the seashore and a crowd gathered to listen to hear what he had to say. Jesus hopped onto a fishing boat so more people could see and hear him.

"Thanks for letting me use your boat," Jesus said. Then he said to the fishing brothers Simon and Andrew, "I want to thank you with lots of fish. Throw out your nets!"

"We'll try," they sighed. Simon and Andrew put their nets into the water. "But we fished all night and caught absolutely nothing," they explained to Jesus.

Suddenly, they felt their nets tug. They were overflowing with fish! Rip! Pop! Snap! The nets were so full that they were breaking. The brothers pulled in so many fish that their boat started to sink. "Help!" they called to their friends in another boat. "We have too many fish!" James and John rushed to their rescue. The weight of the fish almost took their boat under too!

They knew that their new friend, Jesus, must be someone special. He was the one who told them to catch those fish.

"Hey, Simon and Andrew! Hey, James and John! Follow me!" Jesus called to them. "Let's catch people instead of fish." Splash! The two sets of brothers dropped their nets into the sea. They were not fishermen anymore. Now they were disciples! Now they would follow Jesus.

Jesus met a tax collector at his office. "Hey, Matthew! Follow me!" Jesus called. "Let's collect people instead of money." Clink! Matthew the tax collector dropped his coins to the ground. He was not a tax collector anymore. Now he was a disciple! Now he would follow Jesus.

Jesus met seven others that day: Philip, Bartholomew, Thomas, another James, Thaddaeus, another Simon, and Judas. "Follow me!" Jesus said to each of them. Crash! Boing! Boom! They all stopped and dropped what they were doing. Now they were disicples! Now they would follow Jesus!

Jesus and his 12 friends, the disciples, shared the workload with many other followers, including Mary

Magdalene, Joanna, and Susanna. No matter where he went, Jesus called for men and women, boys and girls, to drop what they were doing and follow him.

⭐ Play follow the leader. Take turns being the leader. What kind of leader do you like to follow?

237

# The Beatitudes

News that Jesus was coming had spread all over the town. "Maybe he will make sick people well!" some people thought. "Maybe he will make hurt people walk!" thought others.

Everyone wanted to see Jesus. There were so many people, how would they all be able to see him? Jesus knew. He climbed part way up a mountainside and sat down. Now all of the people could see Jesus. Everyone waited. Someone yelled, "Quiet, I want to listen!" "Sh-h-h," mothers told their children. Then Jesus began to teach the people.

Jesus said, "People who feel hopeless are blessed because God will give them heaven.

Sad people are blessed because God will help them feel better. People who don't have many things are blessed because God will give them everything they need. People who want to follow God's ways are blessed because God will help them. People who treat others with kindness are blessed because God will treat them with kindness.

People who know what is right in their heart are blessed because God will be with them. People who make peace are blessed because they will be called God's children. People who are hurt because they try to do what is right are blessed because God will give them heaven."

Wow! So many blessings! Did Jesus have anything more to tell the people? He did. Jesus told the people, "If other people don't like you and they hurt you, say bad things about you, or tell lies about you because you are my friend, you are blessed! Be happy because God has a special place for you in heaven!"

The crowd became noisy. People were smiling. Jesus had blessed the people. What a happy day!

Think of a time when you have been sad. How did God help you feel better?

# Love Your Enemies

Jesus taught people everywhere about God. Jesus' teachings were different from what people had heard before. This made people curious about what Jesus had to say!

One day Jesus was talking about how to treat your enemies. Jesus said, "If someone hurts you, don't hurt them back." Wow, that was different! Then Jesus

said, "If someone asks you for help, say, 'Sure!'" People hadn't always thought like that before. "And remember to share what you have with other people," he said. Hmmm . . . Jesus had the people thinking.

Then Jesus said a very important thing. "Everyone says, 'Love your friends and hate your enemies.' I say love your enemies and pray for people who are mean to you. This is what really makes God happy!" The things Jesus said changed the way people thought about treating others.

Do you follow what Jesus said about how to treat your enemies? Is it easy or hard to do?

# Do Not Worry

Jesus loved to teach people about how God wants people to live.

"God takes care of us!" Jesus said. "Don't worry about what you are going to eat or what you might wear or when you'll grow taller. God will take care of these things for you. Look at the birds. Do they worry about what they eat? Of course not! God makes sure they have food. Look at the flowers. Do they worry about what color they are? Of course not! God made them each beautiful in their own way. And God makes you beautiful too. You're beautiful simply because you are YOU!"

Then Jesus said, "Listen! There is far more to life than worrying. Worry gets you nowhere—so stop! The one thing you need to do is put God first. Trust that God will take care of you!"

What kinds of things do you sometimes worry about? Who can help you to stop worrying?

245

# The Lord's Prayer

The disciples had seen Jesus do many amazing things—heal the sick, teach in the temple, and pray to God. They wanted to learn everything they could from Jesus. "Teach us to pray," they said to Jesus. Out of all the things Jesus did, they thought this was the most important.

"When you pray," Jesus said, "don't be like the people who stand on the street and use big words, loud voices, and long prayers. Find a place where you can be alone. Then you will think only about God."

Jesus said this prayer to show the disciples how they could pray:

Our Father in heaven, hallowed
be your name, your kingdom come,
your will be done, on earth as in heaven.

Give us today our daily bread.
Forgive us our sins as we forgive
those who sin against us. Save us from
the time of trial and deliver us from evil.

For the kingdom, the power, and the
glory are yours, now and forever.
Amen.

When Jesus said these words, he was saying that God is holy and important here on earth and in heaven too. He was asking God to give him what he needed each day. Jesus was also teaching us to ask God to forgive all of our sins (which God always does!), and help us to learn to forgive other people. He asked God to help him remember to do what's right and not what's wrong. He finished his prayer by saying that everything in the world belongs to God, forever and ever.

Jesus taught the disciples so much about prayer! They never forgot how Jesus told them to pray or the words Jesus used to pray to God.

Make a special prayer place. Go there every day and pray to God.

# House on the Rock

Jesus liked to teach people by telling them stories. Sometimes he told stories called parables. Through parables, people learned God would help them, especially when things were not easy in their lives. Jesus told this parable about two houses to many people as he sat with them on a mountain one day.

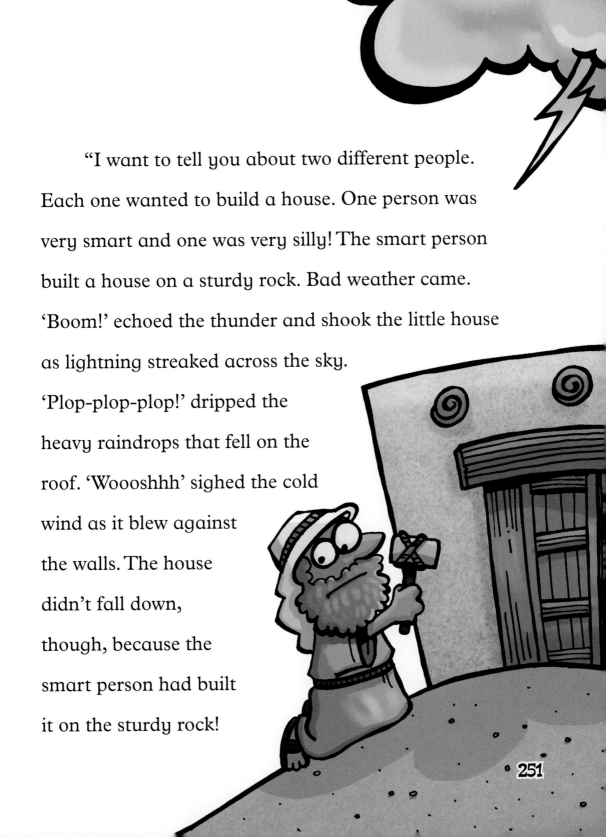

"I want to tell you about two different people. Each one wanted to build a house. One person was very smart and one was very silly! The smart person built a house on a sturdy rock. Bad weather came. 'Boom!' echoed the thunder and shook the little house as lightning streaked across the sky. 'Plop-plop-plop!' dripped the heavy raindrops that fell on the roof. 'Woooshhh' sighed the cold wind as it blew against the walls. The house didn't fall down, though, because the smart person had built it on the sturdy rock!

"The silly person built a house on sand, and something very different happened! Bad weather came. 'Boom' echoed the thunder and shook that little house, too, as lightning streaked across the sky. 'Plop-plop-plop!' dripped the heavy raindrops that fell on the roof. 'Wooooshhh' sighed the cold wind as it blew against the walls. Guess what happened this time? Because the silly person built the house on sand—crash!—it fell down!

"If you listen to me, you are building your life on the sturdy rock of God. If you don't listen to me, you are building your life on ideas that are like the sand that shifts and blows away."

When Jesus finished talking, the people on the mountain were surprised by his words. They had never heard stories like that from their rabbis before. Jesus was a wonderful teacher who helped them learn how to always trust God.

⭐ Who likes to tell you stories? What kinds of stories do they tell you?

# A Storm

Jesus and his friends, the disciples, met by a lake one day. They were going to go fishing together.

Creak, creak. The fishing boat rocked as Jesus put one leg over the side of the boat and pulled himself in. "Follow me!" Jesus said to his disciple friends.

One by one they climbed into the boat. Finally, they pushed off from shore.

Jesus' friends talked and laughed in the boat. They told stories about all the fish they caught on this lake.

"What was your best fishing trip, Jesus?" one of his friends asked. But Jesus did not answer. He was sound asleep. Zzzzzz.

Gray clouds came into the sky and pushed out the sun. The boat rocked harder now. The first raindrops came. Plop. Plop.

255

The disciples held their cloaks around them as the rain fell harder. Brrrrr! The rain was cold, and the wind was blowing strong against their skin.

Waves came over the top of the boat. Splash! Lightning flashed all around the boat. Thunder cracked! Jesus' friends yelled, "We shouldn't be out here on the lake!"

How could Jesus sleep? Flashes of light and gusts of wind came every second. Jesus' friends couldn't wait any longer. They shook Jesus awake. "Help us, Jesus!" they cried.

Jesus opened his eyes and saw the fear on their faces. "Why are you so afraid?" he asked.

Jesus stood up in the boat and lifted his arms. "Peace. Be still." In an instant, waves lay down on the lake. Shhhhh. Clouds made a space for the sun.

The raindrops stopped, and there was silence instead of thunder.

Jesus' friends stared at each other. "Did you see that? Jesus saved us! We're alive. We survived that awful storm. Thank you Jesus!"

Show someone how your face would look before, during, and after the storm if you had been on the boat.

# The Centurion's Servant

Jesus went to visit the people in a town called Capernaum. When he arrived, a large crowd was waiting to see him. A soldier, called a centurion, hurried toward Jesus. The centurion was a powerful man

in charge of many servants and soldiers who did whatever he said. He told Jesus, "My servant can't walk, Lord. I need your help. Please make him well."

Jesus answered, "I will come and heal your servant."

"Thank you, Lord," the centurion said. "You are more powerful than I am, and I believe that you can heal my servant." Jesus was amazed at the centurion's words.

"This man has great faith," Jesus told the people around him. "Go home," Jesus said to the centurion. "Your servant is no longer sick."

The centurion rushed home, where he found his servant healed.

Do you know anyone who is sick or sad? Pray for them.

# The Sower

Jesus sat in a boat
when he told some
people on the shore a
story about a sower who planted
seeds on the ground. Some seeds landed on a path.
Birds came along and ate the seeds, so the plants didn't
grow. Some seeds landed in dirt with lots of rocks. The
sun was too hot and burned those seeds, so the plants

didn't grow. Some seeds landed in dirt with too many weeds. The weeds choked the seeds, so the plants didn't grow. Some seeds landed in good soil, and the plants grew and grew!

Jesus wants us to share God's Word like the sower who scattered the seeds. Just like some of the seeds that didn't grow, some people will not listen to God's Word. But many people will listen, and God's Word will grow in them.

⭐ Plant a seed in a cup. Use good soil. Give it to someone who needs to hear about God's love.

# Walking on Water

The disciples were just waking up on their boat. They had been out on the water all night. Yawn! Stretch! It was so early, the sun wasn't even up yet.

Andrew rubbed his eyes and looked into the fog. "Hey," he whispered. "Do you see what I see?"

"Oooh! It's a ghost!" James cried out in fear. The disciples were shaking in their sandals.

They were terrified. Through the fog, they could see the outline of a person walking on the water.

It was Jesus. "Don't be afraid! It's just me," Jesus said. He waved a friendly hello.

"If it's really you, Jesus, tell me to walk on the water," Peter said bravely.

"Okay!" Jesus shrugged. "Come on out, Peter! The water is fine!"

Gulp! Peter swallowed hard. He placed one foot onto the water.

Plop! It didn't go under! He tried the other foot. Plop!

He was standing! He kept his eyes glued on Jesus as he

took a few careful steps. He walked faster and faster.

Splish! Splash! Only his feet were getting wet. Jesus

smiled at him.

Peter felt the wind blowing on his face.

He took his eyes off of Jesus and looked up

at the dark clouds. He felt afraid.

Uh oh! His ankles were wet. Uh oh!

His knees were wet. Uh oh! Peter was

sinking! "Help me, Jesus! Save me!"

he yelled.

Jesus reached out his hand and

pulled Peter out of the sea. "Why did you

stop looking at me?" Jesus asked, holding

tightly to his friend. "Don't you

trust me?" The wind stopped.

They climbed into the boat full of cheering disciples. "Hooray! This proves it!" they said. "You really are the Son of God!" From that day on, the disciples were excited to tell everyone they met about the power of Jesus.

Would you have been more like James or Peter if you saw a person walking on top of water?

# The Vineyard Workers

Jesus told this story to teach about God.

A farmer needed workers for his vineyard where he grew grapes. "Will you work in my vineyard?" he asked some people.

"How much will you pay?" they answered.

"One day's pay," the farmer said.

"Okay," said the people, and they went to work. The farmer hired other workers at different times all day.

When they were done, the farmer paid all of the workers the same. The first workers were angry!

"You paid the last workers the same as us!" they shouted. "We worked longer in the hot, hot sun!"

The farmer answered, "I gave you what I promised you. Are you upset because I'm being generous to the others?"

Jesus said that God is generous like the farmer. "The last will be first and the first will be last with God," he said.

⭐ **Practice being generous. Let someone take an extra turn in a game or do extra chores at home.**

# The Greatest Commandment

The Pharisees were a group of people who had lots and lots of laws. Altogether they had more than 600! Whew! That's a lot of rules to follow! One day one of the Pharisees said to Jesus, "Teacher, what's the greatest law?" He didn't think Jesus could possibly pick just one law out of so many. He was trying to trick Jesus!

But Jesus knew the man was trying to trick him. He looked at the man and smiled. "Love God with all your heart, and with all your soul, and with all your mind," Jesus said. "This is the greatest of all the commandments. But there's another really important one too.

Love your neighbor as yourself. If you obey these two laws, then you obey all of the laws."

The Pharisees' jaws dropped to the floor. They were shocked to know just how smart Jesus was. They were surprised Jesus had answered their question and turned their trick around on them. They didn't know what to say.

Then Jesus had a question for them. "What do you think about the Messiah? Whose Son is he?" That was an easy question for the Pharisees. They grew up

learning in school that the Messiah came from the family of David, so that's what they told Jesus.

"Then why do all the people from the family of David praise David as the Messiah?" Jesus asked. Now that was a hard question. The Pharisees didn't have an answer. They backed away and didn't trick Jesus again.

How would you feel if you were Jesus and a big group of people tried to trick you?

# Jesus Blesses the Children

272

Jesus traveled all over the land, telling people about the good news of God's love.

One day Jesus was talking to a large crowd. It seemed that there was always a crowd! The children had to stand on their tiptoes or sit on their parent's shoulders just to see Jesus. People were everywhere on the grassy hill—laughing and smiling and waiting for Jesus to tell them more about God.

"God loves you and you and you," Jesus said. "He wants you to love other people too."

One mom said, "I want my children to hear what Jesus is saying!" Other parents wanted their children to hear Jesus too. They moved closer and put their children down on the grass. One small boy tugged on the corner of Jesus' robe—and Jesus turned around.

"Ah," Jesus said smiling, and he bent down to hold the hands of the children standing nearby.

But the disciples scolded the parents. "What do you think you're doing? Jesus is too important and too busy to talk to these children! Move your children back!"

When Jesus heard the disciples say these words, he stood up and turned back to the grown-ups.

"What do you mean?" Jesus said to the disciples. "These children are as important to me as you are!"

275

"I want to bend down and look in their eyes and tell them about God's love too. Never stop anyone from coming to see me, especially children. Let the children come sit on my knee—children like these are a part of God's big family too."

Then Jesus knelt down to look each child in the eye. "Come sit with me," Jesus said, "and I will tell you about the love of God, my Father." Jesus sat on the grass with all the children and told all of the girls and boys about God and God's family. Then Jesus put his hand on every girl's head and every boy's head and blessed them saying, "Remember, God and I love you just the way you are!"

Then Jesus stood up and said to all of the grown-ups, "Remember my words—whoever does not love God like a child won't be part of God's family."

How would you have felt if you had been one of the children Jesus talked to in the story?

# A Rich Man's Questions

A rich man asked Jesus, "What do I have to do for God to love me forever? I think I'm doing everything God wants me to do . . . so will God always love me?"

"Sell everything you have," Jesus said. "Give all that money to the poor. Then come follow me."

The rich man was shocked! Sell *everything*?! He had lots and lots of stuff. He walked away from Jesus.

Jesus said, "It's hard for greedy people to enter the kingdom of God. In fact, it's easier for a lumpy, bumpy camel to walk through the itty, bitty eye of a needle. But, don't forget, for God, *all* things are possible! God loves us always and no matter what. Nothing we do gets us God's love, and there is nothing we can do to lose God's love. It is forever."

279

# Bartimaeus Sees

Jesus did something amazing one day near the town of Jericho! He and his disciples were leaving for Jerusalem with a large group of people. Sitting all alone by the side of the road was a blind beggar named Bartimaeus. He heard the people walking by and talking about Jesus. When Bartimaeus figured out that Jesus was with the crowd, he knew just what to do. He was hoping Jesus could heal his eyes so he could see again. In a very loud voice that everyone could hear, Bartimaeus shouted, "Jesus, please help me!"

Many of the people with Jesus were upset that Bartimaeus was interrupting them and yelled back, "Be quiet!" "Stop bothering Jesus!"

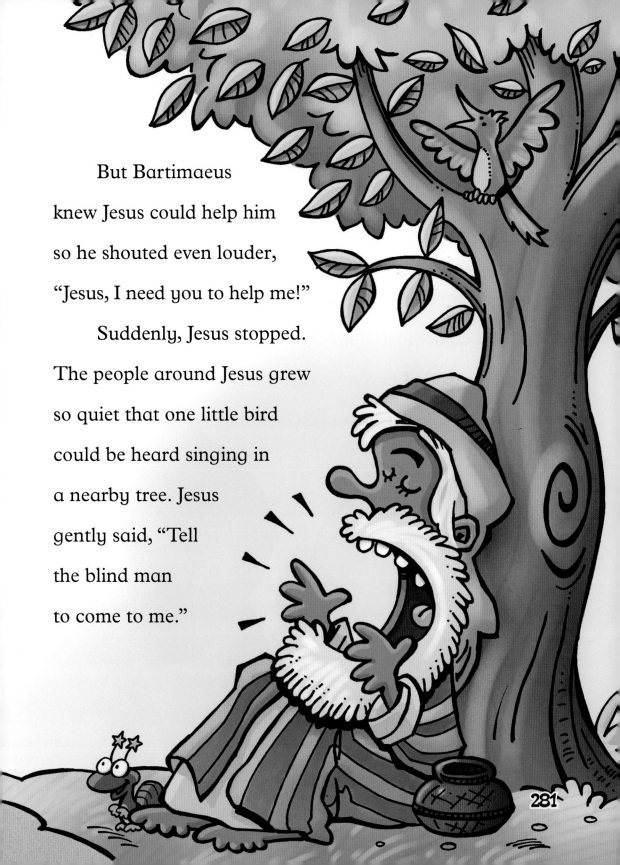

But Bartimaeus knew Jesus could help him so he shouted even louder, "Jesus, I need you to help me!"

Suddenly, Jesus stopped. The people around Jesus grew so quiet that one little bird could be heard singing in a nearby tree. Jesus gently said, "Tell the blind man to come to me."

The crowd called to Bartimaeus, "Get up! Jesus wants to talk to you." Bartimaeus was so excited he threw off his dusty coat, jumped to his feet, and made his way to Jesus.

"What do you want me to do for you?" Jesus asked kindly. Bartimaeus, whose faith in Jesus was very strong, said, "Please help me to see again."

Jesus didn't even need to touch Bartimaeus. In a firm voice Jesus said, "Go, Bartimaeus! Because you

believe in me your eyes are healed."

And right then Bartimaeus could see! He saw Jesus, the crowd of people, even the little bird singing in the tree. Bartimaeus was so happy that he joined the crowd and followed Jesus.

**What is something you can ask Jesus to help with?**

283

# The Widow's Offering

Jesus sat down outside a temple and taught the disciples about how to share.

"Do you see that rich man in fancy robes?" Jesus asked the disciples. They looked around and saw him. He twirled his robes when he saw that they were watching him.

"I must be very special," thought the rich man.

The man in fancy robes stopped in front of a moneybox outside the temple. He slowly reached into his money purse and pulled out several coins. One by one he held them up to the sun so that they flashed for all to see.

"It's time for me to give to the poor!" he said very loudly. The coins made a loud "Clang!" as he dropped them in the moneybox.

Now Jesus asked the disciples another question. "Do you see that poor old widow?" Jesus whispered the question because he didn't want to scare her. She looked this way and that. She tried to hide in the crowd. She bent over the moneybox. "Clink. Clink." Her two tiny coins barely made a sound as she dropped them in. The old woman reached her hand into her pocket. It was empty.

Quietly, the poor woman shuffled away. "Did you notice?" asked Jesus. "The man in fancy robes gave just a little of his riches and showed off a lot. The widow gave the only two coins she had and kept quiet about it.

She shared everything. She is the one who gave the most.

This is how I want you to share."

How does it feel when you get to put your coins in the offering at church?

287

# Four Friends

Jesus met many sick people when he was traveling from place to place. In one town, Jesus was in someone's house teaching people about God. Other people in the town had heard Jesus was a healer, and they were very excited when they found out he was nearby.

Four of the townspeople had a friend who was paralyzed. The four friends knew that if they could just get their sick friend to Jesus, he would be healed. They carried their friend on a stretcher and tried to bring him into the house. But it was so crowded they couldn't get through the door!

"What should we do?" asked one friend.

"Maybe we should just give up and go home," another answered sadly.

"No! I have an idea," said the third. "Let's take our friend up to the roof. Then we can cut a hole in the roof and lower him in!"

"Let's try it!" said the fourth friend.

So, they all climbed up on the house and cut a hole in the roof. Using rope, they slowly and gently lowered their friend into the room where Jesus was teaching.

All of the people in the room were surprised to see a man being lowered from the roof, except for Jesus. Jesus knew the man was paralyzed. Jesus also knew sin hurts people more than sickness. So Jesus did an unusual thing.

Jesus said to the man, "Friend, your sins are forgiven."

291

The people in the room were confused and angry. They thought nobody could forgive sins except God. They didn't know that Jesus was God's Son.

"Don't be angry," Jesus told them. "I am God's Son, and God has given me the power to forgive sins."

Again, the people were confused and surprised. They didn't know if Jesus was telling the truth.

"I am telling the truth," Jesus said. "I can prove I am God's Son."

He turned to the paralyzed man and said, "Friend, stand up."

The man stood up. He had been healed! Now the people were amazed.

The healed man thanked Jesus and carried his stretcher home with his four friends.

Many people believed that Jesus was God's Son, and they praised God that very day. They knew that if they or their friends ever had a need, Jesus would be there to heal them, to forgive their sins, and to love them!

Sit on the floor and pretend you cannot use your legs. How will you walk? Get into a chair? Dance?

# Banquet with Simon

Jesus was invited to dinner at Simon's house. Knock, knock! "Thanks for coming, Jesus!" Simon led his guest through the dark door to a low table. "Dinner is served!"

Jesus was ready to eat his bread when he heard a woman at the door. When she saw Jesus, she started crying. The woman was known to have done many things wrong.

"Please pass the grapes!" Jesus started to eat. Drip, drip, drip. The woman bent over Jesus' feet and cleaned them with her tears.

"Please pass the cheese!" Jesus said. Wipe, wipe, wipe. The woman dried the tears on his feet with her long, dark hair.

Jesus put down his bread. The woman was kissing his feet and rubbing them with oil.

Simon was upset! He said, "I didn't invite that woman! What is she doing?"

295

Jesus cleared his throat and told a story. "One person owed a bank 500 coins. The other person owed 50 coins. The bank canceled the payments for both people. Who was more thankful?"

"The one who owed the most, right?" asked Simon.

Jesus nodded yes. "I'm like the bank," he explained. "I forgive and forget big and little mistakes."

He put his hand on the woman's head. "This woman made many big mistakes. She needs a lot of forgiveness so she shows me great love."

"You're my host, but you didn't greet me as a special guest. You have little mistakes for me to forgive, so you give me only a little love."

"Dry your eyes, my friend. I forgive all you've done wrong," Jesus said to the woman in a kind voice. "You have a strong faith."

Simon learned a lesson that day. All people are important and equal to Jesus. God forgives and forgets mistakes of all sizes.

If Jesus were coming to your house, how would you get ready for his visit?

# The Transfiguration

Peter, James, and John were very excited! They were climbing a mountain with Jesus. Higher and higher they climbed, right to the top! Then they noticed something different about Jesus.

Jesus' face and clothes were bright and shiny like the sun! Moses and the prophet Elijah were standing with Jesus, talking about God's promise to save the world. Peter couldn't believe his eyes!

Suddenly, a cloud covered the mountain. A voice said,

"This is my Son. Listen to him." The voice was God! Peter, James, and John covered their faces. Then Jesus touched them. They peeked up. Everything was the same as it was before—even Jesus.

On the way back down the mountain, Jesus, Peter, James, and John talked about God's promise, but they didn't tell anyone else what happened on the mountain for a long time.

⭐ Look at a cloud in the sky. Imagine hearing God's voice coming from it. What is God saying to you?

# The Good Samaritan

A clever man who thought he knew all the rules
for living God's way asked Jesus a question. He wanted
to see if he could trick Jesus into giving the wrong
answer. "Teacher," he said, "what must I do to live
forever with God?"

Jesus asked another question. "What do the commandments say?"

The man answered, "The commandments say you should love God with everything you have. And you should love your neighbor as much as you love yourself."

Jesus replied, "That's the right answer! Live like this and you'll live with God forever."

"So, Jesus," the man continued, "who's my neighbor?"

Jesus answered the question with a story.

A man was traveling down a scary and rocky road by himself. All of a sudden, a group of men jumped out. They stole his money and hurt him, leaving him by the side of the road. He moaned and groaned in pain. He couldn't get up.

A little while later a priest was going down the road. He saw the hurt man and passed by him on the opposite side of the road. Later, another man came along and passed on the other side of the road too. When a Samaritan came along and saw that the man was hurt, he stopped to help him.

A tear ran down the Samaritan's cheek as he bent down to help the hurt man. He put bandages on the man's cuts. The Samaritan huffed and puffed as he tried to lift the man onto his donkey.

He took the man to the nearest inn and put him in a room. He took care of him for the rest of that day. The next day the Samaritan had to leave for a few days. He paid the innkeeper to take care of the hurt man. The Samaritan promised to return and pay the innkeeper any more money that was needed to care for the man. He wanted the hurt man to get better.

After Jesus finished the story, he asked the clever man, "Which of the three men was a neighbor to the man who was hurt?"

The man replied, "The one who stopped to help him."

Jesus told him, "God wants us to help everyone. People of every size, shape, and color and from every country are important to God. Now, go and be like the Samaritan and help everyone who needs help."

How would you have felt if you were hurt and people who walked by didn't stop to help you?

# Mary and Martha

Jesus and his disciples were traveling. Along the way, Jesus decided they would visit with their friends Mary and Martha. Mary and Martha were sisters. They lived in a house together. They got along very well—most of the time, at least!

While Jesus visited with them, Mary sat on the floor and listened to Jesus teach.

Martha, on the other hand, was very busy. She didn't have time to sit down! She cooked—olives, fish, and bread. She cleaned—sweeping the dirt floor and shaking out mats. Martha worked hard to make Jesus' visit special.

307

As she hurried around, she saw Mary sitting down with Jesus. "Hmmph!" she thought. "Why doesn't she help me with the cleaning?" A few minutes later, Mary was still sitting as Martha worked. Martha got a little bit angry. "A-HEM" she cleared her throat, thinking, "Mary could at least help me get this meal ready! All of these people to feed and she isn't helping one little bit!"

Martha continued hurrying around, getting angrier by the minute. As she swept, she thought, "Rrrrrgh! Mary knows how to use a broom!" As she cooked, she said to herself, "Harrumph! I think my sister could at least stir this pot!" As she got water and towels ready for cleaning Jesus' hands, she grumbled to herself, "Grrr! All of this company, and I am doing all of the work!"

Finally, when she was still working and Mary was still sitting, Martha couldn't take it any more. She burst into the room, interrupted what Jesus was saying, put her hands on her hips, and said angrily, "Mary! PLEASE get up and help me!" She looked at Jesus. "Augh! Jesus, tell Mary to get up and do something!"

Jesus stopped what he was doing. Everything was quiet for a minute. Finally, Jesus looked at Martha. With love, he said, "Martha, Martha! You are worried about every little thing! Thank you for your work to make my visit comfortable, but you do not need to worry about all of those things! Mary has decided to sit and listen to me—and that is a good decision!"

Martha thought to herself, "Hmmm . . . maybe I *should* just sit down and listen to what Jesus has to say, at least for a minute! Maybe Mary has a good idea!"

So she sat and listened—and that was a good decision!

Act a bit like both Mary and Martha— help a grown-up with a chore, then read a Bible story together.

# The Lost Sheep and Lost Coin

Telling stories was Jesus' favorite way to teach people about God.

"Once there was a shepherd who had 100 sheep," Jesus said. "He loved them all—the big ones and the little ones, the good ones and the naughty ones. They were his sheep and he loved them.

"Every day this shepherd counted his sheep to make sure they were all safe. One day he counted only 99 sheep! Oh no! One was missing! Right away, the shepherd left the 99 sheep together and went to look for the one that was lost.

"The shepherd listened for the lost sheep to 'B-a-a.' He looked in all the places that sheep might get stuck or in trouble. It took awhile, but the shepherd kept looking until he found the missing one! Then he called to all of his friends and neighbors. 'Come on over!' he cried. 'I found my sheep! Let's have a party!'"

Jesus loved telling people stories like this about something being lost and then found.

"I have another story," Jesus said. "Once there was a woman who had saved up 10 little silver coins. One day when she was counting them, she discovered that she had lost one. What do you think she did? Did she think to herself 'Oh well—I've still got nine, so who cares if one is lost?'

"No, she did not! She lit her lamp and swept the house from top to bottom. She looked under and over and around *everything* in her house until she found that lost coin! Oh, she was so happy she had a party to celebrate.

"God is like this shepherd and this woman, you know," Jesus said. "God would never stop looking for someone who was lost."

How would you feel if you were lost and then found?

# The Prodigal Son

Jesus spent time with all sorts of people—even people who had done bad things. This made some people mad. "Why is Jesus always around people who do bad things?" they grumbled. Jesus heard them, so he told them this story.

A man had two sons. The younger son, who was a bit wild and crazy, came to his father and said, "Dad, I want to get away from here. I want my money." This made the father sad, but he split his money and gave his son the part that was his. The younger son packed his bag and headed out away from home.

317

The son traveled to a faraway country and spent all his money on fancy parties and food. Soon he had no more money and no place to stay. Lucky for him, he found a man who let him sleep in his barn if the son fed the pigs.

*"What am I thinking"* he said to himself as he fed the pigs. *"The men who work for my father have more than enough to eat and here I am starving to death. I'll go home and say to my father, 'Dad, I made a big mistake. I'm not good enough to be your son, but would you let me work for you?'"* So he went home.

319

While he was still far away from his house, his father saw him. His father ran and threw his arms around him. The father put a ring on his son's finger and shoes on his feet and ordered for a party to be thrown for him. The older son saw his father's servants preparing for the party and asked, "What's going on?"

"Your brother is home," said a servant. "And your father is having a party." This made the older brother angry at his father.

"I have always done what's right," he said to his father. "I've worked hard for you, but you never gave me a party. Now my brother came home after he wasted your money. Why are you throwing him a party?"

"My son, you have always been with me. But your brother left, and has now come back!"

Then the people understood. Jesus spent time with those people because even though they had done bad things, they decided to change their lives and live like God wanted. This made Jesus so happy!

 How would you have felt if you were the younger son, and your father was so happy to see you?

# Ten Men Healed

Jesus was walking toward Jerusalem. As he neared the village, two scared faces popped up from behind the branches of a nearby tree. Three more sad faces peeked out from behind a giant rock. Jesus looked into the distance.

Five more frightened faces stared out from behind a large leafy plant. Ten faces—each covered with red, bumpy spots. Ten men—some missing their fingers and toes—tried to warn Jesus.

"Stay away!" one shouted. "Leprosy!" yelled another. "Keep your distance," another warned.

Jesus knew the men were sick. He felt sad for them. "Jesus!" one man shouted. "Can you heal us?"

"Go! Show yourselves to the priest," Jesus said.

The men stood up and started walking into town.

Suddenly, they stopped.

"Look! Our spots are gone!" one shouted. "Look! Look!" another exclaimed. "My fingers are growing! And my toes are back!"

Soon all the men were jumping up and down with joy. The men ran toward Jerusalem. They would show themselves to the priest. They were healed!

One man turned back to look at Jesus. He threw himself face down on the dusty road. "Thank you, Jesus! Praise God! Thank you!" he said so loudly that the birds flew up in all directions. Jesus laughed to see the man so happy.

But where are the others? Weren't there ten of you?" Jesus asked. "Where are the other nine? Don't they want to praise God too?"

The man did not hear Jesus. He was too busy counting his toes and fingers. Yes, ten of each, just where they should be! Jesus said, "Go, you are well!" The man jumped up and scurried after his friends. His voice filled the morning. "Pra-a-a-ise God!" he shouted as he ran as fast as his ten toes could carry him.

One man stopped to thank Jesus. What are you thankful for? Stop right now and thank God for that gift.

# Zacchaeus

Many people lived in a town called Jericho. One of them was a rich man named Zacchaeus. He had a big house, a big yard, and lots of money! Zacchaeus was rich because of his job. He collected taxes from the people for the Roman leaders. However, Zacchaeus always took *extra* money from the people and kept it for himself! The people did not like Zacchaeus!

Zacchaeus saw a crowd of people gathering along the side of the road and heard someone say, "Jesus is coming!"

"Jesus?" thought Zacchaeus. "Who is Jesus? He must be important. I want to see him too!"

Zacchaeus wanted
to see Jesus, but he had a
problem. Zacchaeus was
short, too short to see Jesus
from the back of the crowd.

He needed to get in front of the taller people, but he knew they didn't like him. "They'll never let me in front," he thought. Then, Zacchaeus had an idea.

He found a tree next to the road where Jesus would walk. The tree was just the right size for Zacchaeus, so Zacchaeus climbed the tree. Now he could see everything!

He could see the road, he could see the crowd, and he could even see Jesus! Zacchaeus got excited. Step, step, step. Jesus came closer and closer until he was right under Zacchaeus's tree. Suddenly, Jesus stopped! He looked up and saw Zacchaeus sitting in the tree. Uh-oh. Was Zacchaeus in trouble? Maybe Jesus didn't like Zacchaeus either!

Jesus started to talk to Zacchaeus. "Zacchaeus, come down from that tree. I want to have dinner at your house today!"

"What?" thought Zacchaeus, "Jesus wants to come to *my* house?" Quickly, Zacchaeus climbed down the tree.

"This way, Jesus," said Zacchaeus. "This is the way to my house."

The crowd grumbled. They were upset! Someone yelled, "How could Jesus go to Zacchaeus's house?"

"Zacchaeus is a bad man!" yelled another.

But Jesus didn't hate Zacchaeus. He went to Zacchaeus's house. While they were eating dinner, Jesus told Zacchaeus, "God wants everyone to be part of God's family and to care for others."

Zacchaeus listened closely. Jesus cared for Zacchaeus! Zacchaeus could care for others! He knew just what to do.

Zacchaeus told Jesus, "I will give back all of the extra money I took from the people. I'll even give back more than I took!" Zacchaeus met Jesus and changed forever. He cared about others!

Think of someone you don't always like. Say a prayer. Ask Jesus to help both of you be more caring.

# Wedding at Cana

Jesus was at a wedding in the town of Cana. Jesus' family and the disciples were there. It was a grand day for a wedding—the sun was shining, and everyone was singing and dancing. It was quite a party, with good food and good wine!

"Mmmm," the guests said to one another. "This is probably the best party we have ever been to!"

Then the wine ran out! Even though the servers shook every wine jar, there was none left. Jesus' mother, Mary, heard the servers tell the person in charge of the party,

"All of the stone jars are empty and the wine is gone!"

"How can this be?" they asked. "The party isn't over yet!"

333

Mary slipped away to find Jesus.

"Jesus," Mary said, "they have run out of wine! Can't you do something?"

"What could I do?" Jesus asked Mary.

But Mary knew Jesus could do something. Mary told the servers, "Do whatever my son, Jesus, tells you to do. I think he can help you."

Jesus looked around. Over by the wall, he saw six large stone jars sitting near the table. Jesus walked over to the servers and said, "Fill these jars with cold water."

The servers hurried to the water pool. Slosh, slosh, slosh—they filled the jars with water. When the jars were full of water up to the brim, the servers told Jesus, "We've done what you asked. The jars are full to the brim with cold water."

"Good," Jesus said. "Now put some into a cup, and give it to the person in charge of the party."

Slosh, slosh, slosh—the servers filled a cup from the stone jar and took it to the person in charge. When he tasted it, he smiled. It was a miracle! The water had turned to wine! This wine was even better than the wine they were serving before. The man in charge took a cup of wine to the groom and gave it to him.

"My friend, taste this! You have kept the best wine until now! Most people serve the best wine first, but you have saved the best for last."

The servers hurried to give everyone the new wine. The music played, and everyone sang and danced. This was Jesus' first miracle, and when his disciples learned of it, they believed that he was God's Son even more than they did before.

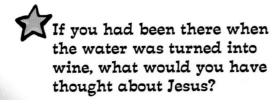

**If you had been there when the water was turned into wine, what would you have thought about Jesus?**

# Woman at the Well

Tired from walking a long way, Jesus rested at a well in a place called Samaria. His disciples went to get food while he rested. The sun was high in the sky. Whew! Jesus was hot. His tongue was as dry as a wad of sheep's wool. He was very thirsty.

A Samaritan woman came to the well to get water. "Will you give me a drink?" Jesus asked. She gave him a puzzled look. Jesus was a Jew, and she knew that most Jews didn't like people from Samaria.

"Why are you asking me for a drink?" she asked.

"If you knew who I was," Jesus answered, "you would ask me for living water."

Now the woman was really puzzled! "Sir," she said as she pointed to the well, "the well is deep and you don't have a jar. Where will you get this living water?"

Jesus smiled. "Everyone who drinks from this well will be thirsty again. But the water I bring lasts forever!"

What the woman didn't understand was that Jesus wasn't talking about water you drink. He was talking about living water—love that forgives and life that lasts forever with God. As Jesus explained more, the woman became more and more interested. She wanted to hear more.

So Jesus told her more . . . lots more. Jesus knew all about her—about where she came from and what she believed.

As they talked, the woman's eyes began to twinkle. "I know the Messiah is coming," she said. "I've heard all about him."

Jesus smiled and put his hand on the woman's shoulder. "I am the Messiah," he said gently. The woman was so surprised; she nearly spilled her water jar!

As the disciples came back with food, the woman rushed past them. She was so excited to tell everyone about what Jesus had said.

The woman ran all over town telling people about what she had seen and heard. "There's a man at the well who says he's the Messiah. He has amazing things

to say! Come and see him for yourself!" she said.

The people came running to see Jesus. Many people believed in Jesus because of what he told them that day.

How would you have felt if Jesus talked to you and he knew everything about you?

# Jesus Feeds 5,000

It was a beautiful, sunny day as Jesus and his

disciples crossed the Sea of Galilee in a boat with white

sails. Jesus had been healing sick people, and many

more people of all ages came to see him again that day.

Maybe they could hear more of Jesus' stories or see him

show God's power through another miracle!

When Jesus saw the large crowd of men, women,

and children he asked his friend, Phillip, "How are we

going to get enough food to feed all of these people?"

Phillip answered, "I could work for six months and not earn enough money to buy food for all of these men, women, and children!"

The disciples didn't know what to do. Just then, Andrew pointed to a young child and said, "Here is a boy who has five small loaves of bread and two fish. It is something, but it certainly isn't enough food for all of these people!"

The boy looked very nervous as he said in a small voice, "Jesus, please take my food if you think it will help."

Jesus took the five loaves of bread and two fish that the boy offered and asked his friends to have the crowd sit down. About 5,000 people sat in the grassy meadow by the lake that day!

After Jesus gave thanks to God he blessed the five loaves of bread and two fish. Then he shared the food with all of the people who were there that day. All 5,000 people ate until they were full!

Then Jesus said, "Now, let's gather up all of the leftovers." And do you know what? There were enough leftover pieces of bread to fill 12 large baskets—more loaves and fishes leftover than the boy had given to Jesus! The disciples shook their heads in disbelief as they struggled to pick up the baskets, heavy with food.

The people saw the full baskets of leftovers and began to understand that something extraordinary had just happened—another miracle!

Jesus smiled as he heard people say, "God must have sent Jesus to us!" It was a day the boy, the disciples, and all of the people would never forget.

If you were the boy who gave Jesus his food that day, what would you tell people about what happened?

349

# The Good Shepherd

Jesus wanted people to know that he would always love them and take care of them. He called himself the "good shepherd" and told people that they were like sheep. Some people didn't understand, so Jesus told them this story.

The little lamb was lost. "Ba-a-a!" said the little lamb. "Ba-a-a-a!" The sun slowly slid out of sight.

The little lamb shivered in the cold night air. "Ba-a-a!" He smelled danger. Nearby, a hungry wolf hid behind a thorny bush. "Ba-a-a!" cried the little lamb. "Ba-a-a!"

Down in the valley, a shepherd guarded his flock of sheep, watching and listening. The animals slept peacefully in the cool, green grass. A small stream delicately danced in the evening breeze. A gust of wind swept across the valley. The shepherd paused.

"Ba-a-a," he heard in the distance. "Ba-a-a-a!" He knew the voice of his little lamb. Even though it was dark, the shepherd started up the rocky path that led toward the lost lamb.

"Don't be afraid," the shepherd called out. "I will find you. I will keep you safe!"

The little lamb heard the shepherd's voice. Slowly, he stumbled down the path. A branch scraped his leg. "Ba-a-a!" he cried. The little lamb was scared. He waited for the shepherd to find him. "Ba-a-a!" he said. "Ba-a-a-a!"

When the shepherd reached the lamb, he gently picked him up and held him close. "There you are," said the shepherd. "I have found you. I will carry you home."

352

After he told this story Jesus said, "See, I am a shepherd, too. Just like a good shepherd cares for each and every sheep in the flock, I care for each and every one of you."

Hide a stuffed animal and ask a "shepherd" to find it. Say "Ba-a-a" when the "shepherd" gets close to it.

353

# Lazarus

Three of Jesus' good friends included a man named Lazarus and his sisters Mary and Martha. Jesus was on a long journey when he found out that Lazarus was dying. It took Jesus a few days to travel to see his sick friend. When Jesus arrived, he saw Lazarus's sister, Martha. She had some sad news.

"Jesus! Lazarus is dead!" cried Martha. "I wish you could have arrived earlier. You might have been able to save him!"

Jesus tried to comfort her. "Martha, don't be sad. Lazarus will live again!" Martha believed what Jesus said.

Then, Lazarus's other sister, Mary, came to greet Jesus. She wished Jesus had come sooner too.

"Jesus, if you had been here, Lazarus might still be alive," she wept. She also believed that Jesus could have healed her brother.

Jesus was sad because Lazarus died, too. He cried and cried. Jesus, Martha, and Mary went to the tomb where Lazarus was buried. Jesus told some people standing there, "Take the stone away from the tomb."

The people were surprised at what Jesus said. Martha reminded Jesus that Lazarus had been dead for four days. They had already made his body ready for burial by wrapping it in special clothes. But Jesus knew what he was doing. He insisted that they open the tomb.

When the heavy stone was rolled away, Jesus said, "Lazarus, come out!" The people were frightened and amazed when Lazarus came out of the tomb. Since his

hands and his feet were all wrapped up in the burial clothes, the people had to help Lazarus. When the people saw Lazarus alive again, they laughed and sang and danced. Many people that day believed Jesus would bring new life to all people.

If you had been friends with Lazarus, how would you feel after he died? How would you feel after you saw him alive again?

# Palm Sunday

"Friends!" Jesus said to his disciples. "I need to go to Jerusalem. I've got some important things to do and I want to celebrate Passover with you there. Will you come with me?"

"Sure!" said the disciples. "Passover is a great holiday! Such good food! And what a wonderful story Passover celebrates—the exodus of God's people, the Israelites, from Egypt! It's good to be with friends and family at Passover." So Jesus and his friends started to go to Jerusalem.

When they got close to the city, Jesus said, "I'd like two of you to go borrow a donkey in the next village over. Please tell the owner I need it. He'll understand."

When the two friends came back with a donkey, Jesus climbed on its back and rode down the hill into the city of Jerusalem. The disciples followed behind him.

Suddenly, they found themselves in a parade!

People were singing and shouting, "Hosanna!

Hosanna! Here comes

God's king! Hosanna!

Praise God!"

People all over heard the shouting and singing and they joined the parade too. Hundreds of people! Thousands of people! They started taking off their coats and laying them on the ground for Jesus and the donkey to walk on. They pulled palm branches down from the trees and waved them as they sang. Then they threw their palms on the ground to make a path for Jesus.

The crowds gave Jesus a royal welcome as he rode into the city, just like a king. But Jesus was a very different king—he was a king of peace. Not everyone understood that. Jesus was not at all what they were expecting.

They thought the crowd was too loud and the parade was getting too big. "Who is that man?" someone asked. "What's going on here?" asked another. The crowd answered, "This is Jesus! God's King! He has come to save us!" Some of the religious leaders

murmured, "Hush! Jesus, tell your friends to be quiet—it's way too loud here!"

But Jesus said, "We can try to make these people be quiet, but that wouldn't make a difference because today the whole earth is celebrating!"

Make your own palm out of green paper and pretend you are in the parade. Shout, "Hosanna! Praise God!"

363

# The Last Supper

Jesus knew that the time had come for him to leave this world. He wanted to share his last Passover meal together with his 12 closest friends, the disciples. Jesus loved his friends and wanted to show them his love in a very caring way.

As the friends got ready for the meal, Jesus put water in a large bowl and knelt down on the floor. He wanted to wash the feet of each disciple. When it was Peter's turn, Peter said to Jesus, "You will never wash my feet!"

Jesus replied, "Peter, you don't understand what I am doing now, but you will later."

Peter loved Jesus so much that he said, "Then don't just wash my feet but my head and hands also!" Peter wanted to be as close to Jesus as possible.

365

As they were eating, Jesus sadly told his disciples, "Soon, one of you will betray me. One of you will tell people who don't like me where I am so they can take me away."

This upset the disciples, and each one said, "It's not me you're talking about, is it?"

When Judas said this, Jesus gently replied, "Yes, Judas, you will betray me."

Then Jesus picked up a loaf of bread. He blessed it and gave some to each of his friends, saying, "Take this bread and eat it. This is my body." Then Jesus picked up a cup of wine. He gave thanks and said, "Drink this. It is my blood which I must give up so the sins of people may be forgiven."

When the meal was over, Jesus and his friends went to a place called the Mount of Olives. Jesus said sadly, "Soon you will all leave me."

Peter felt bad. "Even if all the others leave you, I won't!" he said.

Jesus looked at his dear friend and said quietly, "Before the sun rises, you will pretend you don't know me three times."

Peter said, "Jesus, I love you too much to ever do that to you!"

And all of the other disciples said the same thing.

What can you do to show people that you love them?

# Jesus Is Betrayed

Jesus had a good friend named Peter who was there when Jesus healed people and made miracles happen. Jesus liked Peter so much he gave Peter the nickname "The Rock." Jesus had another friend named Judas.

Jesus, Peter, Judas, and the other disciples spent lots of time together. They were all together when Jesus told them that his life had to end. It was a sad and hard time for Jesus and his friends.

Jesus felt so sad that he went to a quiet place in a garden and prayed. "Please God," Jesus prayed, "make me strong. Help me trust you."

Jesus asked the disciples to come to the garden and stay awake while he prayed. But they fell asleep.

"Wake up. Wake up. Wake up," Jesus told the disciples three times. When Jesus finished praying, it was time for them to go and face hard things.

Even though Jesus had many friends, he had some bad enemies too. Some people were scared that Jesus would change the world too much with love.

Judas got scared too. He let Jesus down. Judas told some of Jesus' enemies where Jesus was. When soldiers came to the garden, Judas kissed Jesus on the cheek to show them who they were looking for. The soldiers took Jesus away. Judas and Peter ran away and hid. They were so scared.

Later, Peter waited outside the place where Jesus was on trial. A girl saw Peter and said, "He's a friend of Jesus. He's in trouble too!" Peter wanted to help his friend Jesus, but he was scared, so he pretended he didn't know Jesus. "I don't know him.

I don't know him. I don't know him," Peter said. His lie made him feel even worse inside.

Peter ran away again. He cried and cried. Peter felt so sad for Jesus. Peter felt very, very sorry.

But Jesus knew that Peter loved him. Jesus knew that Peter was his friend. That's why he had given Peter such a special job. The Rock became a strong leader in the church. He told many, many people about his best friend, Jesus. "I know him. I know him. I know him," Peter told everyone. And THAT was the truth.

Has a friend ever let you down like Peter and Judas? What happened? How did it make you feel?

# The Day Jesus Died

It was a very sad day when Jesus died. The soldiers who had arrested Jesus teased him for pretending to be a king. They took his clothes and put a king's purple cloak on him. They made a crown of vines with sharp thorns and put it on Jesus' head. Ouch!

The soldiers made Jesus carry a heavy wooden cross. The cross was too heavy for him. Jesus fell and skinned his knees, and the cross tumbled to the ground. A man in the crowd carried the cross the rest of the way.

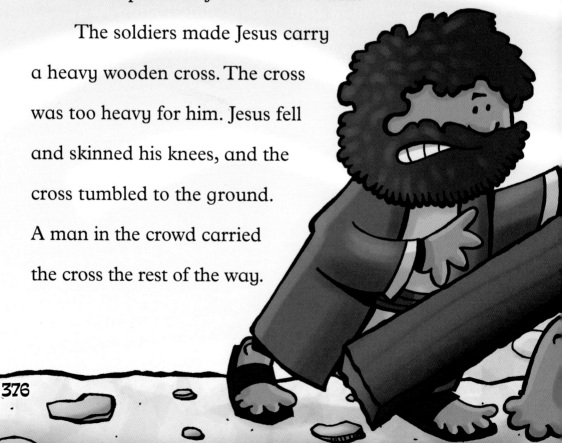

The soldiers nailed Jesus' hands and feet to the cross. They raised Jesus' cross up on a hill between two other men. The other men were thieves and they were being crucified too. One of the men was angry with Jesus.

"If you are a powerful king, can't you save yourself? Why don't you save us too?!" The man spat at Jesus.

But the other thief believed in Jesus. He shouted back, "Don't you know who this is? This is God's Son. He hasn't done anything wrong. We are being punished for our mistakes. But Jesus shouldn't be here."

The man turned to Jesus and asked, "Will you take me to heaven with you?"

Jesus looked at the man and loved him. Jesus told him, "Yes, today we will be in heaven together."

After a while, the world grew very dark, as if a terrible thunderstorm was coming. It was as if all of creation was crying because Jesus was about to die. Jesus was feeling all alone and prayed to see if God was still there. Of course, God never left Jesus. God was with him the whole time.

Jesus looked at the crowd. He was so sad that people didn't believe that he was God's Son. He asked God to forgive them for killing him. The soldiers offered him some sour wine, but he didn't want to drink it.

He was ready to die. Finally, Jesus had fought for long enough. He said, "God, the work you gave me to do here is finished." He breathed a final, long, slow breath, and then he died.

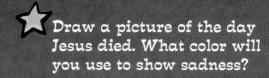 Draw a picture of the day Jesus died. What color will you use to show sadness?

# The Empty Tomb

It was early in the morning on the third day after Jesus died. The sky was pink and red with the first light of the sun. The women didn't notice the sky.

They hurried to the cave that contained Jesus' body. Mary Magdalene and Mary, the mother of James, led the way. Two others, Salome and Joanna, carried the spices to rub on the body of Jesus. They had a job to do.

When the tomb of Jesus came into sight, they froze. Uh oh! They had forgotten about the huge stone that sealed the opening to the cave. How would they move it?

The women kept going to the cave anyway. As they came closer, the women could see that the stone had already been rolled away!

They peeked inside. Ooh! It was dark in there. Brr! It was cold in there. Drip, drop! It was damp in there. What?! It was empty in there! Jesus was gone!

An angel appeared in sparkling white clothes. The glow from the angel brightened even the darkest corners of the cave. The women shielded their eyes from the blinding light. "Don't be afraid!" the angel said. "Jesus isn't here. This is a place for the dead. Jesus is alive!"

"Hurry," the angel said, "go tell the disciples!" The women did not delay. They ran to tell Jesus' friends what they had seen and heard.

Oof! Mary bumped into a man, tripped, and fell at his feet. Wait! She knew those feet. A familiar hand reached out to help her. Wait! She knew that hand. She looked up. Yes, she knew that smile. It was Jesus!

"Hello, friends!" Jesus said. Jesus was really alive! The women hugged his feet and shouted with joy. "Go tell the others the good news that I am alive," Jesus said. "I will meet them in Galilee. I can't wait to see them again!"

The women had a new job to do!

They had to tell everyone Jesus was alive!

⭐ **What would you have done if you were one of the women and saw the angel in the cave?**

387

# The Road to Emmaus

Three days after Jesus died, Cleopas and his friend were slowly walking down the road to Emmaus. They were walking slowly because they felt very sad. "Why did Jesus have to die?" they wondered. After a while, a stranger began to walk along with them. The stranger was really Jesus, but Cleopas and his friend didn't know it.

"What are you talking about?" the stranger asked.

The men looked at each other. "Are you the only person in town who doesn't know what just happened?" they asked. They told the stranger what had happened to Jesus. "Jesus was a great teacher," Cleopas said.

"We hoped he was the one God promised would save the world, but instead he died on a cross! We took Jesus' body down and put it in a tomb. This morning, our friends went to the tomb, but Jesus' body was gone! They said there was an angel there instead! The angel told our friends, 'Jesus is alive,' but . . ."

"Stop being silly!" the stranger said. "How many times do you need to hear this? It was God's plan for Jesus to die and become alive again to save the world!"

By now, they were almost to Emmaus. Cleopas invited the stranger to stay for dinner. During dinner, the stranger picked up a loaf of bread, broke it, blessed it, and gave each man a piece. All of a sudden, Cleopas and his friend recognized the stranger. It was Jesus,

but then Jesus disappeared! Cleopas and his friend jumped up, ran from the room, and went to tell the rest of Jesus' disciples that Jesus really was alive! God kept another promise!

If you saw Jesus walking down the road, who would you tell? What would you say?

# Doubting Thomas

The disciples were hiding in a house the night Jesus rose from the dead. They were afraid. Bam! They locked all the doors. Jesus came and stood by them.

"Peace be with you," he said. The disciples looked up in surprise! Jesus showed them his hands and his side so that they would know it was him. The disciples were very happy! Again, Jesus said to them, "Peace be with you. God has sent me to you. Now it's your turn to go tell the rest of the world about me."

Jesus breathed on them in a very special way. He said, "With this breath, I will always be in your hearts, even when I am in heaven. You now have the power to do the things I've asked you to do."

Thomas was the only disciple not there that night. When he got back, the others excitedly told him about Jesus' visit.

"I don't believe you!" Thomas said. "I'll believe when I can touch Jesus' wounds."

A week later, Thomas and the other disciples were in the same house. Jesus came again and stood with them. "Peace be with you," he said to them.

"Thomas," Jesus commanded. "Come here! Give me your hands. Put your finger on the wounds in my hand. Put your hand by the wound in my side.

Do not doubt anymore. It's time for you to believe."

Thomas' eyes popped. "My Lord and my God!" he exclaimed.

Jesus answered him, "You believe because I'm here with you and you've seen me. Think of those who have not seen me, but believe in me anyway. You should believe, even when you cannot see it for yourself."

Act out the story of a time when you were afraid, but you felt Jesus was with you.

# The Great Commission

Jesus went to see the disciples after he had been raised from the dead. They buzzed with excitement. "Is that you, Jesus?" "We're so glad to see you!" "Do you want something to eat?"

Jesus smiled. "Peace be with you!" he said. "I have things to tell you!" The disciples gathered close around Jesus, eager to listen to him.

Jesus began, "God has given me all the power in heaven and earth."

The disciples looked at each other and began chattering again. "Whoa!" "Wonderful!" "We knew it!" "Fantastic!" "What will you do first?"

"Wait!" Jesus said. "There's more!" The disciples listened

carefully. "Go everywhere in the world and teach people about me. And remember, I will always be with you!"

Jesus returned to heaven. The happy disciples soon began the work Jesus had told them to do.

What would you have done if you were in the room when Jesus appeared to the disciples?

# The Ascension

After Jesus died and rose again, he and his disciples got together near Jerusalem. Jesus had some instructions for them.

"As you know, God is doing amazing things in the world," he said. "And your help is needed! We need you to go tell stories about me! Tell your friends and family and everyone you meet what you've learned by following me! Be my witnesses in the world!"

Then suddenly Jesus was rising—up in the air! What was going on?! He was being lifted up into a cloud!

Jesus' friends looked around. Two men in white robes had joined them. The men said, "Why are you just standing around looking up toward heaven? Don't worry, Jesus will come back some day."

"Right!" said one of Jesus' disciples, "Meanwhile, we have some work to do! Let's get going!"

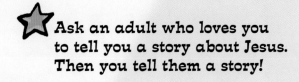
Ask an adult who loves you to tell you a story about Jesus. Then you tell them a story!

# The Holy Spirit

Jesus' disciples were celebrating a festival called Pentecost when suddenly a strong wind blew through the house. Everyone's hair lifted up and there was an amazing noise! They looked at each other. It looked like each disciple had a flame of fire touching him, but no one was burned. The Holy Spirit had come, just as Jesus promised! The disciples began to speak in

different languages! Languages they'd never learned!
Stranger yet—they could understand each other!

Peter stood up. "I want to tell you about Jesus."
He reminded everyone what Jesus taught them. He
told them how Jesus died and lives again. "It's time for
us to begin a new life with God's Spirit guiding us,"
Peter said. The disciples were excited to live differently,
guided by God's Spirit. This was the very beginning of
the Christian church.

Learn to say "thank you" in different languages.

# Early Believers

Some of the early believers were great at sharing. They shared their food and their clothes. They shared their money and their homes. They were so generous! No one was poor or needy because others gave without holding anything back. Together they saw many miracles and wonders. They met in the temple and they met in their homes.

They talked about Jesus and they thanked God for blessing them.

Then something amazing happened. When other people saw how happy these first believers were, sharing all they had and talking about Jesus, they believed too. They became Christians, and they shared their food and their clothes, their money and their homes. They became one big Christian family. And their church family grew and grew and grew.

Try sharing your happiness with others!
Think of something happy or exciting to
tell three friends or family members.

# Peter Heals

At three o'clock one afternoon, Peter and John were walking to the temple together to pray. Ahead of them they saw some people carrying a man who could not walk. They carried him to the beautiful gate of the temple, laid him down, and left him alone.

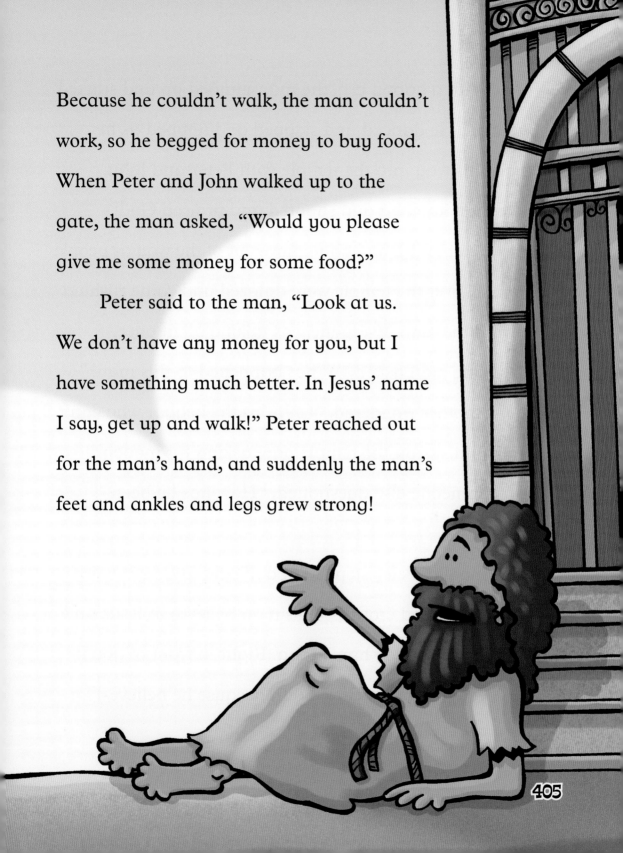

Because he couldn't walk, the man couldn't work, so he begged for money to buy food. When Peter and John walked up to the gate, the man asked, "Would you please give me some money for some food?"

Peter said to the man, "Look at us. We don't have any money for you, but I have something much better. In Jesus' name I say, get up and walk!" Peter reached out for the man's hand, and suddenly the man's feet and ankles and legs grew strong!

With a happy cry, the man jumped up and started walking. He danced and skipped and hopped as he made his way into the temple with Peter and John. The man laughed and shouted and praised God!

Peter and John had to move out of the way as people from all over the temple were amazed and came rushing toward the man. Everyone was talking all at once.

One man asked, "What happened to this man?"

Another wondered, "Isn't this the beggar who can't walk and sits by the temple gate asking for money?"

Someone else questioned, "How has he been healed?"

Finally, Peter stepped in and said in a loud voice to the surprised crowd, "This man believes in Jesus and his faith has made him strong. Right in front of you he has been given a healthy body because he believes!"

Draw a picture of the beautiful gate by the temple. Decorate it with glitter, sequins, or gold and silver crayons.

407

# Saul to Paul

Saul was a bully, and he hated anyone who was a Christian. Saul wanted all Christians thrown in jail. But God had other plans for Saul. Even though Saul was a mean person, God loved him and had a big surprise for him!

Saul had been ordered to go to Damascus. He smiled slyly to himself. If any Christians lived in Damascus, he would find them. He would arrest them and bring them back to Jerusalem. Saul smiled confidently. He had arrested Christians a hundred times before and he could do it again.

Suddenly, swirls of dust blew up from the road. Saul covered his eyes with his arm. "Storms coming up," he shouted to his men.

Crash! Flash! Ka-bash! Saul fell to the ground. A blinding light exploded around him, and a strong voice spoke to him. "Saul, Saul—why do you hurt me?"

Saul rubbed his eyes. He couldn't see anyone. "Who are you?" Saul stuttered.

"I am Jesus," the voice said. "I am not dead. I am very much alive and I have plans for you. Go into the town and wait."

Saul and his men were speechless. They could hear the voice, but they couldn't see anyone. Saul waved his hand in front of his face. "My eyes! I can't see! Someone get me up!" Saul ordered.

Because he could not see, Saul's men led him by the hand into Damascus. There Saul waited and prayed. He wasn't mean or bad any more. God had touched Saul's heart.

A man named Ananias was in Damascus. Ananias loved Jesus. God told Ananias to go to Saul and pray so that he might see again.

"But, Lord!" Ananias said. "Saul is a mean man. I'm afraid of him."

God said to Ananias, "I have chosen Saul to bring my story to many people. I have a plan for him."

Ananias found Saul just as God had said. Ananias prayed for Saul and Saul was filled with God's Holy Spirit. Suddenly, Saul could see again. Ananias told Saul that God had a job for him. Saul was to tell people about Jesus.

Saul was baptized and his name was changed to Paul. Paul served God for the rest of his life. He became a friend of Jesus and told many people how Jesus changed his heart.

Pretend you are Saul. Shut your eyes. Have a friend carefully lead you around your house or yard. Switch places.

# An Angel Frees Peter

Poor Peter! King Herod had Peter arrested and put in chains with many soldiers guarding him. "No one will get Peter with so many guards," said King Herod. Peter's friends gathered at Mary's house and prayed for Peter. Peter was sleeping between two guards when suddenly he was surrounded by a bright light! An angel tapped Peter on the shoulder, waking him up. "Clink, clank" went Peter's chains as he raised his arms to cover his eyes from the light.

"Get up, put on your sandals and cloak, and follow me," the angel told Peter. Ka-clink! The chains fell off of Peter's wrists. He put on his sandals and cloak and followed the angel out of the prison, passing all the guards, who were fast asleep.

415

"Am I dreaming?" thought Peter.

Once Peter was safely away from the prison, the angel left him.

Peter walked to the door of Mary's house. Knock, knock, knock. "Please let me in," Peter said. His friend Rhoda came to answer the door. "I know that voice," she thought. Rhoda was so happy, she forgot to open the door!

416

Instead, she ran back to tell the others who was there.

"Peter is at the door!" she exclaimed. "Peter can't be at the door. He's in prison," they replied. "You must be very tired and you're hearing things."

Peter was still outside the house. He tried again. Knock, knock, knock. Rhoda ran back to open the door. Everyone was amazed! Peter told what happened to him and asked them to tell everyone else the good news.

In the morning no one at the prison knew what had happened to Peter. The guards were in big trouble!

How would you have felt if you were Peter following an angel past all of the guards?

# Lydia

Paul traveled to many places, teaching people about Jesus. One night God told Paul, "Go to another country and teach people there!" Paul listened to God. He got onto a big boat. Up and down, over the waves the boat went, sailing to a faraway country.

When he got there, Paul taught. "Jesus loves you!" he said. "Jesus came to earth to teach us how to live and has saved us all from our sins!"

An amazing woman named Lydia heard Paul teaching. Unlike many other women of that time, Lydia had her own business. She sold beautiful, expensive purple cloth to rich and famous people.

Lydia said to Paul, "Tell me more about Jesus! I want to learn everything I can about the Son of God!"

Paul told her about Jesus' teachings. "Love everyone!" he said. "Share with others!" he continued. "And, most importantly," he finished, "remember that God loves you forever!"

Lydia was amazed. "I want to be one of Jesus' followers!" she exclaimed. "Will you baptize me and everyone who lives in my house?"

Lydia, Paul, and all of the people who lived in Lydia's house went to the water. They splashed into the cool wetness. Paul baptized each of them. "I baptize you in the name of the Father, and of the Son, and of the Holy Spirit!"

Lydia said, "Thank you! Will you stay at my house with my family?"

Paul said, "Sure!" and went to stay with Lydia.

Lydia became a follower of Jesus. She was very generous, using her money to help many people. "Jesus loves you!" she told as many people as she could. "Jesus has saved you from your sins! Follow Jesus—he is the Son of God!"

Many people learned from Lydia, the amazing woman who sold purple cloth.

⭐ Find some purple cloth or scarves. Do a dance of joy for God's love, waving the cloth as you move.

# Paul and Silas

Paul and his friend Silas traveled all over telling people about God. Sometimes people were happy to hear them. But sometimes people grumbled, "Who do they think they are? God isn't like they say!"

422

One day, town leaders grabbed the pair and started to make fun of them. "The things you're saying are lies! How do you know that Jesus is the Son of God? Bah, away with you!"

Paul and Silas were arrested and thrown into jail. It was a very dark night, but they weren't afraid, not one little bit. They knew God was with them.

Paul and Silas prayed, sang, and clapped their hands late into the night. Until suddenly . . . RUMBLE! RUMBLE! CRASH! There was a huge earthquake! It shook the jail so hard the doors opened and the chains fell off the prisoners. The earthquake woke the jailer, who quickly ran to the jail. When he got there, he called, "Is anyone still here?"

Paul yelled out, "Don't worry! We're all here." It was then the jailer knew that God was good and Paul and Silas were good people. They didn't leave when they had the chance.

He wanted to know more, so he asked Paul, "I want to believe in God! How can I be saved?"

Paul told him all about Jesus. "If you believe," Paul said, "then you will be saved." The jailer believed.

To thank them, the jailer took Paul and Silas home and fed them. In the morning, the leaders apologized to Paul and Silas for arresting them and let them go. Once again, Paul and Silas traveled all over, telling people about God.

Do you think it was easy or hard for Paul and Silas to stay in jail after the earthquake? Why?

# Paul's Letters

Paul's job as an apostle was to tell the story of Jesus to everyone he met. He traveled all over his part of the world and started many churches with people who believed in Jesus. When Paul could not travel to visit his friends in Rome, he wrote them a letter to share God's love.

Dear Christians in Rome,

There are three things I tell people who have never heard of Jesus or God:

1. Jesus was human (like us!) *and* God. Both at the same time!

2. Jesus came so people in the world would know how much God loves us!

3. Believing in Jesus and knowing God's love changes your life!

Everyone should know this good news! Are you telling people this good news too?

The peace of God be with you,

Paul

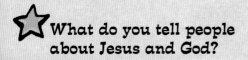 **What do you tell people about Jesus and God?**

# Many Members, One Body

Apostles like Paul stayed very busy telling as many people as possible about Jesus and his love for them. Sometimes Paul traveled to share the good news in person. Sometimes he sent letters to teach his friends more about what it meant to be Christian. Together, they were part of a new family of people who believed in Jesus.

Paul wrote this message to Christians who lived in the city of Corinth. He wanted to help them understand how special the church was, including everyone in it.

"The church is like a human body. One body has many different parts, but it's still one body. We are many different kinds of people, but we're still one body of believers. If a foot said, 'Because I'm not a hand I'm not a part of this body,' that would be silly!

It would still be a part of the body. And if the whole body was an eye, how could it hear or smell?

That's silly too! God made our bodies to have lots of parts, and each part has something special to do. God made all of our parts to work together! The body of believers is the same.

"God has given each of you special things to do. Some of you travel to share the news about Jesus, and some of you teach right where you live. Some of you heal the sick or become church leaders. Is everyone a teacher? Is everyone a leader? No, that would be silly too. God made us to be different and to do different things to show our love for Jesus. Just like the different parts of one body, we all have different talents and we all work together. God has made each of us very special!"

Act out ways of helping others and see if people can guess what you are doing.

# Love Is . . .

Paul's friends in Corinth had lots of good ideas, but sometimes they forgot what was most important . . . love. Paul wanted to help them remember.

Paul said, "If I use words that everyone understands, but don't have love, I'm just a clanging bell or a booming drum making noise.

"If I teach people about God, know what will happen tomorrow, know everything there is to know, and can figure out the mysteries of the world but I don't know about love, none of the other things I know matters. If I sell everything I have and give the money to the poor, but don't have love, I have nothing . . . nothing at all."

"Love is easygoing and kind. It never wants what it can't have. It doesn't brag. It's not rude. It's not selfish. It doesn't get angry, and it always forgives. Love is happy with the truth. Love always protects, trusts, and hopes. Love doesn't give up. It never fails.

"All the things we know and all the things we have will go away some day, but God's love will never go away. Every day that we grow older we learn more and more. Today we only know a tiny little bit about God's love.

But someday we'll know all there is to know about it!"

Paul ended his letter by telling the people in Corinth that love is the most important thing they have. Paul said, "Until the time you know everything about God's love, you have three things to remember: faith, hope, and love. The most important of these three things is love."

☆ How do you know you are loved by others? What does it feel like? Why is love so important?

# Fruit of the Spirit

Paul helped people understand how to live the way God wanted them to live. One time Paul wrote a letter to a group of people called the Galatians. The Galatians had a new church and they needed lots of help!

One of the problems they had was that they were always arguing. They fought and fought about all sorts of things. The Galatians didn't always agree about what it meant to be a church and what rules to follow. They had a hard time getting along, and it was getting in the way of them making a good church! Paul wrote a letter to the Galatians to tell them to stop fighting. He had some great advice.

"To the Galatians," the letter said. "I am so happy that you believe in Jesus, but all your fighting is getting in the way! You're not living the way the Holy Spirit tells you to live. I have a suggestion to try. Instead of living like you are, live with the fruit of the Spirit in mind. Show love, joy, peace, and patience to one another. Be kind, generous, and faithful. And remember, be gentle with one another and always show good self-control. Live with the fruit of the Spirit in mind! That's the way the Holy Spirit wants you to live."

The Galatians looked at each other. They were very quiet. Paul was right. They weren't living the way the Holy Spirit wanted them to! What were they thinking? All this fighting was just not right!

At the end of his letter Paul wrote, "The way for you to get along and be a church is to let God's love fill you. May the grace of God be with you, Paul."

Each day the Galatians tried to remember the words of Paul's letter. They said yes to peace, no to fighting, yes to kindness, no to anger, yes to being generous, no to being greedy. Little by little the Galatians saw God's love and showed it to others. They felt loved by God and they loved each other.

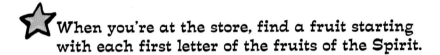 When you're at the store, find a fruit starting with each first letter of the fruits of the Spirit.

# Paul and the Philippians

Paul told many people in many places about Jesus. Some people didn't like it. Sometimes they locked Paul in jail because they thought he would cause trouble. Even while he was in jail, Paul told people his story and wrote letters to his friends.

Many of Paul's friends lived in Philippi. Because they lived in Philippi, they were called Philippians. When Paul was in jail, these friends worried about him. "How could something bad happen to Paul? Wasn't God with him?"

Paul sent a letter to the Philippians from jail with some wonderful news. "Can you believe it?" he wrote. "God is working even here!"

Paul loved the Philippians. He prayed for them and encouraged them to trust God in all things.

Even in jail, God was with Paul. God promises to be with you, too, wherever you are.

How many different places can you think of where God is with you?

# List of Stories and Scripture References